SUDDENLY ALONE

SUDDENLY ALONE

by

Catherine A. Wannamaker, CLA

Equity Enterprises, Inc.
Sarasota, Florida

Copyright © 1998 by Catherine A. Wannamaker

All rights reserved

Cartoons by Bob Donovan, Tampa, Florida

Editing and page layout by Patricia A. Glasnap, Pages in a Snap, Inc., Safety Harbor, Florida

Cover by Foster & Foster, Fairfield, Iowa

Printed in the United States of America

Library of Congress Cataloging-in-Publication Data

Wannamaker, Cather A., 1926-
    Suddenly Alone/Catherine A. Wannamaker. -- 1st ed.
    p. cm.
    Includes index.
    ISBN 0-9645615-1-4

2 3 4 5 6 7 8 9 10

1. Single people — Life skills guides. 2. Divorced people — Life skills guides. 3. Widows — Life skills guides. 4. Widowers — Life skills guides. I. Title.

HQ800.W56 1998   306.88
                                QB197-40702

In memory of my brother
John P. Almon
With thanks for being
there whenever I needed you.

Contents

Preface

Introduction 1

Chapter 1   Safety and Security 7

Chapter 2   Records 17

Chapter 3   Financial Statements 29

Chapter 4   Investments 41

Chapter 5   Insurance 57

Chapter 6   Memories 71

Chapter 7   Retirement 81

Chapter 8   Retirement — Story 93

Chapter 9   Loans 99

Chapter 10   Credit Cards and
                         Credit Rating 113

Chapter 11   Legal Services 123

Chapter 12   Contracts 141

Chapter 13   Estate Planning 147

Chapter 14   Wills and Living Wills 163

Contents

Chapter 15	Final Arrangements	177
Chapter 16	Probate	187
Chapter 17	Divorce	195
Chapter 18	Cookie Jar Money	205
Chapter 19	Medical and Health	209
Chapter 20	Scams	221
Chapter 21	Taxes	239
Chapter 22	Bankruptcy	249
Chapter 23	Prenuptial Agreements	255
Chapter 24	Co-habitation Agreements	269
Conclusion		277
Glossary		281
Index		295

Preface

If you are reading this preface, you are already a candidate for reaping the benefits of Catherine Wannamaker's efforts in drafting this book. In fact, you are reading this preface, you are likely further ahead in your inquiry than most others left "suddenly alone," including Ms. Wannamaker herself a few years ago.

You may have heard of Catherine's history in this field, or read her previous book, *Divorce: A Practical Guide*. There she discusses her transformation from being "uninformed" to being a champion of her own cause and eventually the causes of many others. She knows first hand the dangers of being "uninformed" and the many routes to alter that predicament through the acquisition of knowledge.

Suddenly Alone is an extraordinary guide for the uninformed. I also find it an excellent handbook for the informed who need reminding of the myriad of concerns facing those who find themselves suddenly alone.

Whether by death, divorce, or permanent incapacity of a loved one, a person upon whom you relied in a myriad of concerns has now disappeared. The decisions in life are now yours alone. Even the choice of professionals to help you may constitute decisions of far greater magnitude than you are sufficiently prepared and informed to make.

If you are still with your life partner, you need to make decisions jointly which will affect your lives together and in the future. Catherine shares excellent suggestions for couples in communication about, and decision making, on issues which will have a significant impact on your eventual life alone — as a survivor.

If you have selected this book, then you are the kind of person who wishes to become informed. You are ready to prepare yourself for decisions which will affect your immediate future and your long term plans.

As a lawyer who handles probate administration, inheritance litigation, and family law matters, I often meet with folks who have found themselves suddenly alone. Occasionally I am one of the first calls a person makes after the death of a loved one. Certainly there are legal decisions which must be made and actions which can be taken by an attorney at this time. However, they pale in comparison to the multitude of concerns which arise for which an attorney or other professional would be simply superfluous.

Catherine Wannamaker has codified these areas of concern. Her suggestions will help you make decisions in areas where professional advice is unnecessary, and will help you decide when it is important to obtain professional advice. This is an easily readable text, with logically arranged contents, a helpful glossary, and many forms and examples with which the reader can identify. Catherine has provided her readers a bridge not only to knowledge, but also to the self confidence and assurance which come with being aware of one's own environment.

Catherine has created a book to which I can point many of my clients and say, "Read this, and you will then be prepared to work with your attorney, your accountant, your financial advisor, your insurance agent, and anyone else whom you choose to support you in your new life."

Many of us believe that in every loss lies an unprecedented opportunity. This book will help those left "suddenly alone" secure the opportunities concealed within their loss. It is a way to inform yourself for the trials which lie before you. It is a way to strengthen yourself for the challenges which lie ahead.

Stephen F. Ellis
Attorney at Law
Sarasota, Florida

INTRODUCTION

*

INTRODUCTION

I remember a few years back when a friend and her husband retired to Florida. Her husband of 40 years always took care of the money. After the move, he told her she must learn to handle money, and he handed the checkbook and the finances over to her. She made her mistakes and he helped her through them. I remember her telling me, "I learned you had to put money into a checking account before you could write a check." Now her husband is gone and she is surviving. Without his former guidance, she knows she would have depended on others to take care of her. Because of his foresight, she handles the finances and investments by herself.

Discussing bank statements, final arrangements, money investments, and wills may not be romantic or the topic of the day, but if you are about to be married or if you are married it is vital. Marriage is a financial partnership as well as a loving and social partnership. Neither party should be uninformed about the financial situation of their marriage. Spouses that have little or no knowledge about their family finances could be setting themselves up for financial disaster.

It may seem easier to let him handle all the finances and trust him completely. You weren't gullible, but you just didn't ask. Or, maybe she writes all the bills and handles the investments. Either way, it may come back

INTRODUCTION

to haunt you some day. **When, *if*, one of you will end up alone. You must know about money**. You must know who you owe, where your income comes from, what money is invested, what you own, what arrangements must be made, who to contact, what insurance you or your spouse own and who are the beneficiaries, etc. **Do you know?**

Possibly you have been in a "significant other" type situation. Again the parting promotes some of the same feelings you find in legal marriages. In this type of relationship you do not have the survivorship rights of a marriage. A funeral or divorce that finalizes a marriage or a family relationship is not an option for you. You are left alone, but you have no financial rights unless arrangements have been made before hand. If you don't protect yourself, no one else will.

This book is devoted to the financial and practical problems you may face. This includes: what you can do to prepare and organize, what you must do when final arrangements fall on your shoulders, and what to do when you must put your life back together again. It will also encompass some of the legal procedures you must go through and sometimes it will touch on the very emotional problems you will face. Remember, this is not a book of legal or emotional advice. You must contact an attorney for the legal and a counselor for the emotional. Again there are experts for that. Nothing provided in this book is meant to take the place of, or substitute for, competent legal counsel. It is a book of financial know-how and survival advice from one who has gone through the experience.

I will cover the steps that you can take now with your spouse, your family, your significant other, or whoever is the closest. I will use the pronoun he rather than always he/she, not because I am a woman, but because it is more understandable that way. And even more important, I will cover how you, man or woman, can protect yourself. Work and plan now to avoid the hurried decisions later.

Another friend lost his wife when she was 42 years old. The pain and the anger inside him at the injustice of his situation took over his life. Her part of the joint income was lost, the bills piled up and he was emotionally drained. She handled the finances and he never bothered to find out what the debts were, what bills to pay and when. The worst part was coping with all the immediate and future decisions. They were young and never talked about this possibility. Now it was all in his hands; the children, the money, and the aloneness. It was just too much!

This is what this book is all about. I realize that it is a hard subject to face. Hopefully, you will have a chance to sit down with your lifemate and discuss both of your financial futures. It will happen to all of us and the plans you have made and information you have gathered will strengthen you and help to make you stronger.

Loss of a partner whether it is by death, divorce, or even through permanent disability is devastating emotionally, financially, and socially. This loss, by whatever means, is one of the most stressful experiences anyone will ever go through. The grief, the frightening feelings, the insecurity, and the loneliness are all there. The question you ask yourself is, "How can I survive?"

However, being left alone is not the end of the world. There is a whole new life out there for you. You will survive. You only need to meet it head on. It is the be-

INTRODUCTION

ginning of a new rewarding and gratifying part of your existence.

Whether you are a widow or widower, you must experience the sudden facts that your partner is gone permanently. You are left alone and nothing is going to change that fact. There is no way to bring the person back, no way to again touch their warm living bodies or souls. The emotional feelings will always be a part of you. Unfortunately, it leaves you in a changed financial situation that you must learn to deal with. All that is left is the legal work and the financial exchange of ownership. The survivor of any relationship must work with what is available and go on from there.

In the case of divorce, it is a little different. The partner is lost, but the hope that it is not over is always there. Not only is there grief and other feelings, but also a feeling of guilt and/or rejection. The legal proceeding of a divorce will change the current financial picture. No matter what the judge or the parties do, there will not be enough money for both of you to live the way you have been accustomed. You will have to adjust to the present circumstances.

If this separation is because of another reason, such as disability, a whole different set of problems arises. You are still alone and the financial burden is on your shoulders. Maybe it is more than you can handle. Look around and contact an appropriate support group. The support group will know where to get help and ways for you to cope.

It is surprising how many wives do not know how much their husbands make and vice versa. There is a naivete on the part of one spouse not knowing the total income of a marriage. Many times one spouse makes out the yearly income tax or has it prepared and the other signs it without reading it. The same is true of the assets and liabilities of the marriage. Start now to discover your position financially. Talk to your spouse.

If you are alone now, this book will give you the knowledge to help you survive. Read the book, think about the information and use this information to build a more secure and wonderful life. Set your goals and follow them. Open up this new world and let the sun shine down on you.

CHAPTER 1

✳

SAFETY AND SECURITY

SAFETY AND SECURITY

This chapter is devoted to your safety and security. Safety and security are usually used interchangeably. But, for basic understanding in this chapter, the words will be used with different connotations and with different definitions.

SAFETY:
Physical danger protection; mental awareness of a possible peril; free from danger, defense of person; averting possible criminal acts; any device or act for preventing accidents. (Personal danger)

SECURITY:
Loss or damage to possessions, assets, protection and/or avoidance of potential criminal acts against your belongings. (Things)

While you are part of a couple, there has always been the other person available to help protect you from harm. When you are alone, you are completely responsible for your own safety and security. Will you be safe? Are you able to protect what belongs to you? That is up to you. Remember, nothing is more important than you or your family's physical safety.
Not money! Not your home! Nothing!

SAFETY AND SECURITY

PERSONAL AND PHYSICAL SAFETY:
Each and every one of us must go out into the streets and our community. Some of us travel to far away places. Wherever we go, there is possible danger. Take a few preliminary precautions and make them habits. Prevention must be practiced until it becomes a natural part of your everyday life.

- ✓ Put good locks on doors and keep them locked when you are alone or away from home.
- ✓ Make sure you have a smoke detector and that it is in working order. Check the detector at least once each year. (Plan to do this on your birthday month.)
- ✓ Use a motion detector and a timed light so you won't come home to a dark house.
- ✓ If you have a garage door, install a garage door opener with a reverse feature. This will allow access to the garage without getting out of the car. Make sure the garage light automatically goes on when the door is opened.
- ✓ Work out an arrangement with a friend to check on each other.
- ✓ If you are mugged, always give them all your money, purse, package, etc. Immediately get to a safe place and then report the incident to the police. Don't hesitate or give the robbers any chance to take additional action.
- ✓ A con artist or criminal can look like your friendly banker or even like the nice person next door.
- ✓ Keep your eyes and ears open and always be aware of your surroundings and what the people near you are doing.
- ✓ Mobile phones — keep the charger near your bed. Put the phone there each night. This way you have

a phone close if there is a problem in your home or with the regular phone line. It can then be used for both incoming and outgoing calls from any part of the house.

WALKING:
- ◆ Always present the appearance of knowing exactly where you are and where you are going. Walk assertively and keep your hands free except for your car key. Don't talk to strangers when you are out on the street. Avoid wearing visibly expensive jewelry and carrying large sums of cash.
- ◆ Make sure, if you need directions, to go to a well lighted and populated area. Unless absolutely necessary, don't ask someone out on the road or sidewalk when you are alone.

AUTOMOBILE:
- ◆ Put all your valuables in the trunk of your car before leaving home and before parking the car.
- ◆ Always park in a well-lighted area. If you must go out at night, try to have a companion or an escort walk you to your car. Mall areas can be dangerous, both day and night. If you are out late, make sure there are others around before walking to the car. Find a security guard to walk you to your car or to stand outside until you are inside your automobile with your doors locked.
- ◆ Before going to your automobile, take out the car door key. Carry it in your hand with the point out. It will be ready to open the door quickly and can act as a weapon if needed. If you are attacked, don't be shy. Use the key on the attacker's eyes. Protect

SAFETY AND SECURITY

yourself! You will only have one chance to surprise your attacker.
◆ Never try to walk to your car with both hands occupied carrying your purse or packages. You need your hands free for quick action.
◆ Lock all the doors as soon as you get in your car. Do this before organizing your purse and other purchases. Start the engine immediately so, if necessary, you can drive away quickly. As soon as you are able, put the seat belt on. (For women, hook the strap of your purse in the seat belt.) Never drive without the seat belt, except in an emergency.
◆ At night, if you are approached by a red light of a possible police car asking you to pull over, signal them that you will take the next well lighted, populated area to stop. Drive slowly. Let them know you are not trying to outrun them.
◆ Hitchhikers are just asking for trouble. You don't need to be a good samaritan. If the hitchhiker seems to be from a disabled car, go to the next available phone and notify the police for assistance.
◆ No matter how quick an errand is, never leave the car motor running when you are out of the car.
◆ When having your car repaired, give only the car key to the mechanic. Keep all other keys with you.
◆ Keep some small change in your car as well as in your pocket. It is difficult to make a phone call for help if you don't have change. Be sure to have the necessary tools for disabling times. (Tire jack, spare tire, rain gear, extra shoes, flashlight, etc.)
◆ Keep the car's maintenance up and never let the gas tank get below a quarter of a tank. Check your owner's manual for information. Inflate your tires

correctly for fuel economy and safety. Rotate tires every 8,000 miles, check alignment twice a year, inspect tires for cracks, and bulges or uneven wear.

ACCIDENTS:

Automobile collisions, even minor ones, can cause a lot of trouble and money. It is advisable after an accident, no matter how minor, to follow several basic rules:

- ◆ Do not get out of the car except in an emergency unless there are other people around. Think of your own injuries, if any, and your safety first.
- ◆ Call the police even though there is only minor damage and no personal injury.
- ◆ Don't talk too much. **Even if you are responsible for the accident, don't say anything.**
- ◆ Count the number of people in the other car(s) immediately. Get their names, addresses and telephone numbers. Make a notation if you believe they have an injury. Some people will put in a claim even though they were never in the car.
- ◆ Jot down the full name of the driver, address, driver's licence number, insurance company name and policy number, telephone, and car licence. Check the registration, and if the name is different, write that name down also.
- ◆ Look around to see if there are any witnesses. List their names, addresses, telephone numbers and make a notation on what they saw.
- ◆ Jot down licence numbers and states, names, telephone numbers, addresses of any witness or person involved.
- ◆ List the name(s) and badge number(s) of the policemen investigating the accident.

SAFETY AND SECURITY

- It is a good idea to carry a disposable camera in the car. If you have one, take pictures of the car, the injuries, and even of the area around the accident. If you do not have a camera, take time to write an account of the accident, road conditions, weather, time and date.
- See a doctor immediately in the event of an injury. Don't wait until a question of injury comes up.
- Call your insurance agent and report the accident. You can discuss the accident with the agent even if you do not file a claim.

> **Hint:** *Put a copy of this list in the glove compartment of your car.*

RESTROOMS:
- Don't go to a restroom that is out of the traffic area or sight of people. Make sure it is well lighted and accessible. When traveling, it is always safe to stop at a McDonald's (they are clean and wheel chair accessible) or most other restaurants. Most will allow this without a purchase.
- Always hang your coat, purse, or camera on the lower hook of a restroom door or hold onto them. Never throw a coat over the door or lay a package or purse on the floor.
- Keep one eye on valuables when washing hands or during grooming. Never walk away and leave anything on a counter or table.

SECURITY TO POSSESSIONS:
Many of the basic safety precautions were listed in the section on safety. Besides protecting yourself, you

need to develop habits that will protect what you have worked hard to attain.

Home:
- ◆ Keep doors locked while you are home and when you are out.
- ◆ Check windows to see they can be opened and still not allow possible entry from outside. Block any sliding windows with a dowel in the window track to allow only the opening you desire.
- ◆ Sliding glass patio doors should have lock protection as well as protection for a small ventilation opening.
- ◆ Be sure you identify all persons before allowing them in your home. Don't let a strange person into your home to use the phone. Offer to make the call for them.
- ◆ Do not obstruct the view from the windows.
- ◆ Keep emergency phone numbers next to **all** telephones. It is a good idea to have more than one telephone available in the house.
- ◆ Always make appointments for repair persons. If necessary, recall the company to make sure of the time and person coming. Always check their identification before admitting them to your home.
- ◆ Install motion detectors on the corners of your home to light up dark areas.
- ◆ Plant thorny bushes or plants below your windows.
- ◆ Halogen bulbs: Keep away from curtains and children, only use recommended bulb size, operate at a lower setting if possible and

SAFETY AND SECURITY

never leave lamp set at high when left unattended or when leaving home.

Cash (ATM) Machines:
- Pick the area for the ATM machine that you will use. Avoid using machines in mall parking lots.
- Avoid areas with hedges or any other hiding places where a stranger can be concealed. Check for monitoring cameras that record the transactions and use these locations.
- Never use an ATM after dark without having someone with you; have all forms filled out and ready. This will shorten your time at the ATM.
- Stay alert and be aware of anyone trying to watch your transaction. Never write your pin (code number) on anything you carry. Memorize this number. If you are using a drive through, allow the person ahead of you to pull away before driving ahead. (Don't let yourself be blocked in).
- Never give pin, Social Security number, or bank account number to anyone calling you on the phone.
- Treat your ATM card like cash. Save all receipts. Report a stolen card immediately.

Sales and Maintenance People:
- Watch any information you give them; be careful when writing a check or when showing your identification.
- Unless you know the sales or maintenance person, never allow the person to be alone in the house.

- ◆ Check the identification of anyone coming into the house for repairs, sales, etc. This is true for utility people as well.

TRAVEL:
- ◆ Prepare a list for the person watching your home. This list should include alarm system, location of important papers, travel intentions, who to notify in case of an emergency, etc.
- ◆ Always carry your prescription medications on your person.
- ◆ Stop mail and newspaper delivery.

ROBBERS LOOK FOR:
- ◆ Unlocked doors or windows.
- ◆ A note left on the door.
- ◆ A key left in a handy place, under the door mat, in the mailbox, over the molding of the door, etc.
- ◆ An unanswered phone. Never leave a message on the answering machine that you are out. Always say something to the effect that you are unavailable, can't get to the phone, busy, etc.
- ◆ Papers left in the driveway.
- ◆ Open garage doors.

CHAPTER

2

✳

RECORDS

RECORDS

Every individual collects records and they become part of the quilt of our lives. Take time to assemble this quilt of records both in document form and from your mind. Protect yourself with knowledge as well as protecting those that survive you. Locating and documenting in the time of crises is not only difficult, but sometimes impossible.

Give your survivors the information and the location of any and all records before it becomes necessary. Let them know what your desires are and how you want them to handle your affairs. Nothing is worse than muddling through a crisis without knowing where vital information is and what is needed.

Start today locating this information. Go through your files, safety deposit box, desk drawers and any other place your records might be located. Now is the time to locate or obtain all records. Put them together with your notes and, **please**, tell somebody where to find them when needed.

FORM # 1:
List most of the vital records needed in the case of any emergency. Take time to copy the form (at the end of this chapter) and check each record you have. Make

Records

notes on the copy for each item checked and the location of these records. Not only will this organize your records but will organize yourself about your current situation. Start today and get your affairs organized:

- ◆ Names, addresses, telephone numbers, relationships of all-important people. Be sure to include family, friends, lawyer, accountant, clergy, etc.
- ◆ Medical:
    1. Doctor's name and telephone numbers and the condition the doctor is treating.
    2. Medical insurance company name, address and telephone number, policy number, premium amount and premium due dates.
    3. List all chronic health problems as well as the name and dosage of any medication you are taking.
    4. Nursing or an extended health care policy company name, address, telephone number and policy number.
    5. Organ donor card. Tell someone where this form can be found. It is not necessary that everything on it is discussed with your survivors, but they do need to know how to locate all documents immediately.
- ◆ Birth, marriage, death, baptism, Bar Mitzvah, confirmation certificates.
- ◆ Important numbers:
    1. Social Security number and location of card.
    2. Driver's license number, state, renewal date.
    3. Veteran's Administration number and which VA holds the records.
    4. Military discharge (DD214), any documents pertaining to military service.

- Credit Cards: type and name, account number, addresses of company, telephone number, credit limit, balance, interest charged, who can use these cards.
- Insurance policies: name, address, policy number, due date and premium amount of each
    1. Home: Type of policy, policy number, coverage.
    2. Life: Face value, whose's life, beneficiary, alternate beneficiary, owner, type of policy.
    3. Vehicles: Coverage, liability, telephone number of the agent, covered drivers.
    4. Other: Disability, umbrella coverage, travel, accident etc.
- Employment records:
    1. Wages: Name and address of the employer, pay-stubs, length of service, bonuses, benefit papers etc.
    2. Self-employed: Nature of business, location, where records are kept, past tax records.
    3. Corporation: If you are the owner of the corporation, you will be receiving a salary. The same records are needed as self-employed. Also add the location of the shares you own for this company and names and telephone numbers of all other shareholders.
- Trusts: Type, location of documents, beneficiaries, alternate trustee.
- Retirement accounts: Owner, type of retirement account, company name and address holding funds, current value, when benefits payable, beneficiary.
    1. Pensions: Amount and is there a survivor benefit? Check the benefits booklet.

Records

2. 401(k), IRA, SEP: Interest and/or mutual fund investment.
- Deeds: Home, timeshares, vacation homes, rentals you own, real estate investment property.
- Mortgage: Name of the financial institution or individual holding the mortgage, location, amount due, amount of interest charged. (Include last real estate tax information.)
- Lease or rental agreements: Include not only living area but, cars, boats, equipment etc.
- Titles for all vehicles: Automobiles, boats, motorcycles, motor home, etc.
- Bank and money market accounts: Location (name and address), account numbers, names on accounts, average balance in each account, purpose of each account.
- Investments: Type and name of investment, location, number of account or certificate, names on accounts for all stocks, bonds, CD's etc.
- Outstanding notes receivable or payable: To or from whom, address, balance and interest charged.
- Debts: List any debts not already covered previously with names, addresses, telephone numbers, amount on each debt, etc.
- Tax returns: Both Federal and state, for at least the last three years along with all verification receipts or documents.
- Pertinent canceled checks and/or receipts. (mortgage, investments, major purchases, etc.)
- Personal and business accounting records.
- Passport: Name, number, renewal date.
- Religious affiliation.
- Antenuptial or postnuptial agreements.

- Child support documents and receipts or record of payment.
- Education: Yours, your spouse, and children.
- Wills:
    1. Regular current will. (See Chapter 14 "Wills and Living Wills")
    2. Living will.
    3. Durable Power of Attorney.
- Safe deposit box or boxes: Location, number of the box, keys out and location, list of contents, names of who has access. Keep in a safe deposit box only items to be secured. Unless there is someone that has immediate access to the box do not put originals of will, life insurance policies, durable power of attorney, living will, trust documents, cemetery deed, etc. Even then some banks will not allow access to your survivor if you are deceased. Check with your local bank for their rules.
- Organizations: Fraternal, religious, social, business.

As you can see, there are a lot of records needed to maintain your lifestyle. You will not have all of the ones mentioned in this chapter and, maybe, you will have others. Hopefully this will trigger your memory to put your affairs in order. It will be easier for you and for anyone coming after you.

FORM #2:
Form #2 (at the end of this chapter) is asking about your personal preferences and ideas. This will give your family a guideline if you become ill or even incapacitated. It may seem too personal but, so is your life and

What makes you laugh? _____
What makes you cry? _____
What goals do you have for the future? _____
_____

What frightens or upsets you? _____
What will be important to you when you are dying?
(i.e. physical comfort, pain, family present.) _____
_____

Where would you prefer to die? _____
How do you feel about life-sustaining measures? ___
_____

Terminal illness? _____
Coma? _____
Irreversible chronic illness? _____
Final arrangements: What are your wishes concerning your funeral and burial? _____
_____

Have you made final arrangements? If so, with whom?
_____

What is your religion? _____
Do you want a religious funeral service and what type? _____
Do you have any favorite hymns or songs? _____
_____

Add any other comments you feel are necessary. ___
_____
_____

RECORDS

Individual Wants and Needs
(Form #2, Copy this form.)

Health:

How do you feel about your current health? _____
_____

If you have a medical problem, does it affect your abilities to function. If so, how? _____
_____
_____

Do you have a doctor? _____
Do you think your doctor should make a final decision about medical treatments you might need? ____
_____
_____

If you could not make your own decisions, would you be willing to let others make decisions for you? If so, who? _____
Do you expect your family to support your decisions about medical treatment? _____
Have you made any arrangement for you family or friends to make medical decisions for you? If so, who and have they agreed? _____
Do you have an alternate person to make the decisions? _____

Personal:

Activities you enjoy. _____
_____

25

Necessary Records
(Form #1, Copy this form.)

- ☐ Addresses of necessary persons
- ☐ Doctors names and addresses
- ☐ Medical insurance
- ☐ Extended health insurance
- ☐ Health problems
- ☐ Organ donor card
- ☐ Vital record certificates
- ☐ Social Security card and number
- ☐ Driver's license (state and number)
- ☐ Veteran's Administration number
- ☐ Military discharge records (DD214)
- ☐ List of credit cards and numbers
- ☐ Insurance policies (life, auto, home etc.)
- ☐ Personal accounting
- ☐ Employment records
- ☐ Self-employment, partnership, corporation
- ☐ Trusts
- ☐ Retirement accounts
- ☐ Pension records and booklets
- ☐ Deed for home
- ☐ Other real estate deeds
- ☐ Mortgages
- ☐ Lease or rental agreements
- ☐ Titles for all vehicles
- ☐ Bank and money market accounts
- ☐ Investments
- ☐ Notes receivable/payable
- ☐ Debts
- ☐ Income tax records
- ☐ Canceled checks and receipts
- ☐ Passport
- ☐ Religious
- ☐ Pre/post nuptial agreement
- ☐ Education
- ☐ Will
- ☐ Living will
- ☐ Durable Power of Attorney
- ☐ Safe deposit box(es) and keys
- ☐ Fraternal organizations
- ☐ Funeral instructions
- ☐ Power of Attorney

RECORDS

your family's love. Help them to help you if it ever becomes necessary.

FORM #3:

Form #3 (at the end of this chapter) lists personal information. Use this form in your estate planning. Take a copy to your attorney and accountant for their records. Make it quickly accessible to your survivors.

RECORDS

Personal Information
(Form #3, Copy this form.)

NAME: _____
              Last   First   M   Maiden or other names

RESIDENCE: _____
                  Street   Apartment   number

_____
             City   State   Zipcode

HOME TELEPHONE: _____
WORK TELEPHONE: _____
SOCIAL SECURITY NUMBER: _____
SEX: Male   Female
BIRTH: _____
            Date   City   State   (Street if known)

OCCUPATION(S): _____

_____

EMPLOYER: _____

_____

PREVIOUS MAIN EMPLOYERS: _____

_____

BROTHERS/SISTERS: Address   Age   Phone

_____

_____

_____

_____

Suddenly Alone

CHILDREN: Birth   Address   Phone

_____

_____

SPOUSE: _____
           Last   First   M   (Maiden or other names)

SOCIAL SECURITY NUMBER: _____

SEX: Male   Female

BIRTH: _____
          Date   City   State   (Street if known)

OCCUPATION(S): _____

_____

EMPLOYER: _____

_____

PREVIOUS MAIN EMPLOYERS: _____

_____

BROTHERS/SISTERS: Address   Age   Phone

_____

_____

_____

_____

_____

REMARKS: _____

_____

_____

_____

_____

_____

_____

CHAPTER

3

✼

FINANCIAL STATEMENTS

FINANCIAL STATEMENTS

In every marriage or significant other relationship, it is vital to know the financial status. This is discovered through the completion of a "financial statement." It is a way of following the process of money as it built and spent and as a guideline to your financial stability.

Completion of a financial statement involves making a thorough and complete analysis of your income, expenses, assets and liabilities. Sample financial forms are included at the end of this chapter. Use them as a model for your own statement.

◆ Begin by listing the monthly income coming into your possession. Copy Form #1 (end of the chapter) and list all income coming into your home whether it is yours, your spouses or your significant other. If one of you is getting alimony or child support, be sure to include this information.

Your income can include wages, commissions, self-employment income, unemployment, Workers' Compensation, rental, interest, dividends, pensions, Social Security, etc. Total all these to figure the amount per month you receive.

Deduct from this the amount taken out for Social Security and the amount withheld for Federal tax. If self employed, allow for Social Security and taxes that will be due or paid quarterly.

Financial Statements

◆ Next, it's time to list all your living expenses. Again, this must be a monthly figure.

> **HINT:** *Be sure the Federal withholding tax is the figure for the amount of income and not the excess to be received later as a refund.*

In the Form #2 sample at the end of the chapter, there are different suggested living costs. Remember, these are guidelines and you may have some that are not there. Add them to the bottom. Be realistic in your figures. Don't go overboard, but then again, make sure you have all your expenses listed.

It is a good idea to go back over the last year or two in your check register to pick up expenses that you can't remember. For semiannual or quarterly payments, annualize them, and then divide by twelve (12) to get a monthly amount. Look at past credit card statements to find what you bought and allow for this in future purchases. Include all your expenses, no matter how frivolous or impractical they were.

Starting at the top, work all figures to an average monthly amount. Be as accurate as you can. Put down what you actually spend, not what you would like to spend.

HOUSING: Use the monthly amount you pay for renting or buying. Some places have a monthly maintenance fee besides the mortgage payment. Add that to the figure.

UTILITIES: Use your check register. Add all the amounts for electricity, water, sewer, garbage disposal, etc. for the past full twelve (12) months and divide by twelve (12) to get a monthly average. If your electricity is already on a monthly average, use that figure.

HEATING/AIR CONDITIONING: If your heating and air conditioning come in your electricity bill, do not use this line. If not, add the cost of oil or gas.

TELEPHONE: The telephone service monthly average includes the monthly charge as well as long distance calls to family and friends.

FOOD: This is the most difficult. Not all of this will be in your check register. Come up with an in-house cost. For outside costs, consider the quick stops at fast food places, as well as regular restaurants. Don't forget lunch money for everyone in the family, as well as the costs for organizational lunches or dinner meetings.

INSURANCE: Average all costs to a monthly amount.
> **Home:** This could be homeowner's or renter's insurance
> **Medical:** Include cost: through work, extra policies, cancer policy, dental policy, etc.
> **Life:** Include cost: through work, personal policies, children's policies, credit union, accident, mortgage insurance, etc.
> **Other:** Disability, credit card loss, mortgage, etc.

MEDICAL:
> **Doctor:** Allow for the yearly deductible, and the amount not paid by insurance company.
> **Dentist:** This must include regular check ups, orthodontists, dental visits, cleaning, etc.
> **Drugs:** Add prescriptions, over the counter medications, vitamins, bandaids, etc.
> **Other:** Don't forget transportation for medical treatment, therapy, hearing aides, glasses, etc.

Financial Statements

TRANSPORTATION:
  Vehicle insurance: Annualize all premiums and divide by 12. Include motor club membership.
  Gas: Estimate as best you can the weekly cost for all cars in the family. Multiply by 52 and divide by 12 to get the monthly figure.
  Maintenance: Again you must estimate, depending on the age of the car, tires, batteries, washing, and waxing.
  Car Payment: Add here all monthly vehicle payments. Make a note on the interest percentage you are paying.

CLOTHING:
  Yours: Add the work clothes you are buying now, plus all other dress and regular clothes. Add to this the amount you spend on accessories.
  Children: School, dress, and play clothes, shoes, accessories, sewing material, and notions. **BE** realistic, but be sure to allow what you really spend.
  Spouse: Figure both work and regular clothing.

CHILD CARE: Care while you are at work, day-care school, after school care and care while you take part in social activities.

EDUCATION: Your night courses, children's private school tuition, continuing education courses, college expenses, books, fees, etc.

RECREATION: Movies, theater, concerts, vacation, games.

MISCELLANEOUS: Children's allowances, gifts, cards, weddings, and baby showers.

PERSONAL: Cosmetics, beauty parlor, barbershop, grooming.

OTHER: Pet care and food, donations, church.

Remember all of this is a projection and may vary a little in exact figures. It's a list of the financial and economic outlook for the future.

> **HINT:** *It is a good idea to go back over the last year or two in your check register and credit card statements for expenditures. Be sure to allow for **CASH** expenditures.*

◆ Next, it is time to figure out what it will cost to live if you are suddenly alone. Use a second Form #2 and take each figure and adjust it to your living apart from the spouse. As a rule of thumb, it takes about 2/3 of the amount it takes for two to live.

If you do not intend to stay in your present home, take time to look for an alternate place to live. You can use that figure to fill in on the cost of a home.

Insurance for health coverage will change unless the coverage is from your work. Check to see if you might be entitled to health benefits from spouse's work. If you use the COBRA law, the cost will go up. Depending on the reason you are alone, you might have to pay this cost yourself.

Will you have a car? Will you be making payments on it? What will the insurance cost be when you are alone?

Possibly you will be going out into the workforce. This will require different clothes for the office/workplace. Allow for this on your financial statement.

If you plan to go on to school, or to do any

Financial Statements

training for future employment, add this to your statement. Do your research, and find out the costs involved.

◆ The next section of the financial statement, Form #3 (end of chapter), deals with the assets the two of you own at the present time, and if they are separate or marital property. Assets are everything the two of you own whether they are titled separately, jointly, or not titled and whether they are tangible or intangible.

List all assets including real property, personal property, automobiles, jewelry, business, stocks, life insurance, pension plans, bank accounts, retirement accounts, etc. Be specific as to the value. This is where it becomes important to have accurate appraisals from a professional. Apply a money value to all assets.

List everything just as you did for your expenses. Do not take into consideration the amount owed on them. Just use either the purchase price or the current fair market value.

Start with what are called liquid assets. This can be the cash in the bank, or the cash in the top drawer. It's anything that can easily be turned into ready cash, such as stocks, bonds, etc.

Next list assets that are harder to convert to cash, such as your home, cars, real estate, limited partnerships, jewelry, collections, etc.

Last is the list of hidden or deferred assets. This will include items such as the cash value of insurance, IRA's, pensions, 401ks, trusts, etc.

Each party might have different assets, and you will need time and patience to find all of them.

Look at past income tax records to see where the income comes from, sales that have been made, rentals, depreciation, etc.

> **HINT:** *This must be as accurate as possible, so it can be used for the distribution of assets if necessary.*

◆ Liabilities are everything you owe to anyone for anything. List all debts, including mortgage, equity loans, second mortgages, bank loans, personal loans, credit cards, family loans, business loans, school loans, car loans, automobile leases, etc.

List them separately in the first column just as you did the assets. Make a note next to the asset if it is covered by insurance. Take the total for the assets, subtract the total liabilities, and it will equal your net worth.

> **Hint:** *You want to keep any notes to remind you how you arrived at the figures in the financial statement.*

Do the same asset and liability statement for yourself and include only the assets and liabilities you will retain if you become suddenly alone.

FINANCIAL STATEMENTS

FINANCIAL STATEMENT
(Make a copy-Form #1.)

Income

Monthly gross wage		$ _____
Deductions:		
Federal income tax	$ _____	
State income tax	_____	
Social Security	_____	
Total	$ _____	
Adjusted gross wage		$ _____
Miscellaneous deductions:		
Health insurance	_____	
Dental insurance	_____	
Life insurance	_____	
Savings	_____	
Loan payments	_____	
Pension plans	_____	
Other (list)	_____	
Total	$ _____	
Monthly wage net		$ _____
Itemize other income:		
Business	_____	
Second job	_____	
Interest	_____	
Investments	_____	
Trusts	_____	
Tax-free bonds	_____	
Tax-free investments	_____	
Limited partnerships	_____	
Other	_____	
Total other income		$ _____
Total monthly income		$ _____

Monthly Expenses

Home rent or mortgage payment $ _____
Housing repair and maintenance   _____
Real estate taxes/intangible taxes   _____
Special assessments   _____
Home insurance/rental insurance   _____
Appliance repair/contracts   _____
Electricity   _____
Heating fuel   _____
Telephone   _____
TV cable   _____
Water & sewer   _____
Pest control   _____
Food: Groceries   _____
         Milk & dairy products   _____
         Special diets   _____
         Lunches   _____
         Meals out   _____
                         Total food   _____
Your clothing   _____
Uniforms   _____
Children's clothing   _____
Laundry/dry cleaning   _____
Medical
         Doctors   _____
         Dentists   _____
         Insurance   _____
         Orthodontist   _____
         Medicine, drugs, vitamins   _____
         Glasses, hearing aids, etc.   _____
                         Total medical   _____
Life insurance   _____
Entertainment   _____
Gifts   _____
Newspapers/books/magazines   _____
Cosmetics   _____
Beauty parlor/barber   _____

FINANCIAL STATEMENTS

Pet supplies _____
Professional & fraternal dues _____
Church _____
Transportation _____
    Gas _____
    Tires _____
    Repairs _____
  Payments _____
  Insurance _____
  Bus/taxi/auto club dues _____
  License _____
            Total transportation _____
Your education _____
Children's education _____
Recreation _____
Vacation _____
Charitable contributions _____
Payments on past Credit Card debt _____
TOTAL MONTHLY EXPENSES $_____

Summary
NET INCOME	$_____
TOTAL EXPENSES	$_____
MONTHLY NET	$_____

Short term debt: Balance   Payment
  Furniture _____ _____
  Credit cards _____ _____
  Loans _____ _____
  Medical _____ _____
  Other _____ _____
    Total short term debt $ _____
Long term debt:
  Mortgage on home _____ _____
  Auto _____ _____
  Business _____ _____
  Other _____ _____
    Total long term debt $ _____

NET WORTH STATEMENT

ASSETS: Value
Cash on hand   _____
Cash in banks   _____
Certificates of Deposit   _____
Stocks/bonds   _____
Notes Receivable   _____
Real estate:
    Home: _____ _____
    Other   _____ _____
Automobiles: _____ _____
                           _____ _____
                           _____ _____

Other personal property: _____
    Contents of home   _____
    Jewelry   _____
    Insurance surrender value _____
Other assets: _____
                           _____
                           _____

TOTAL ASSETS: $_____

LIABILITIES:
Creditor   Security   Balance
_____   _____   _____
_____   _____   _____
_____   _____   _____
TOTAL: $_____ $_____

NET WORTH:
TOTAL ASSETS $ _____
TOTAL LIABILITIES $ _____
    YOUR NET WORTH $ _____

CHAPTER

4

✷

INVESTMENTS

INVESTMENTS

Investing encompasses all stages of the life cycle. You must plan for births, for college, for marriage, for retirement, for death, for divorce, and even for disability. Start now to organize and plan for all life cycles. This particular chapter will give you information to help you and your family prepare for the many life cycles and for when one of you is left alone.

Take time now to make out a financial statement and a net worth statement. This will give you a starting point to work toward the future. If you have made one out before, some items may not change. Others will need to be transferred, cashed, sold, or given away. Compare this statement and net worth to the one made before. Are there items missing? If so, are they gone permanently or are they eventually retrievable?

Make lists of what needs to be changed immediately, what is missing, what you want to change, and what you want to stay the same. These lists will give you a guideline for future planning. To these lists add other vital goals you want to achieve, such as making a new will, moving, health care, retirement plans, etc.

After an up-to-date financial statement is prepared, it is time to look at your investment goals and objectives. While you are working, whether you are looking for both short-term interest or long-term profits, each

investment decision is important. Do your research before making any decision.
- ◆ Define your specific investment objectives and concerns.
- ◆ Define your current tax bracket and how you anticipate the investment will impact your bracket.
- ◆ Decide if you are the type to let unnecessary emotions control your investments.
- ◆ Determine how much you can afford to invest.
- ◆ Determine the effect your proposed investment will have on your long term plan.

HELP AVAILABLE:

There are qualified people to help you plan for your financial future. They have knowledge, information, and research tools. Use them to your advantage and learn from them. Question anything that doesn't seem right and remember, if it sounds too good to be true it usually isn't true.

When you are vulnerable and unknowledgeable, it is easy for others to take advantage. Financial advisors must be paid in one way or another. If you are not knowledgeable about investing, working with a financial planner may be to your advantage. Check out two or three planners; their credentials, backgrounds and the company they work for. Know how the planner you choose is paid. Payment is made by:
- ◆ Variable fee — by the hour, a flat fee, or a percentage based on the assets they manage.
- ◆ Commissions — by the sales made and paid by the firms whose products they sell.
- ◆ Combination — commission for his products, fee for the basic financial advice.

- ◆ Certified Financial Planners (CFP): This certification is issued by the non governmental Certified Financial Planner Board of Standards in Denver, Colorado. A CFP must complete a 10-hour exam and agree to abide by a code of ethics.
- ◆ Chartered Financial Analyst (CFA): Prestigious credential primarily for professional institutional managers and stock analyst. It is issued after several years of work experience and tested by the Association for Investment Management and Research.

> **HINT:** *Financial planning is a convenient cover for fraud. Check qualifications, licenses, education, and Better Business Bureau before investing.*

- ◆ Chartered Life Underwriter (CLU): Held mostly by life insurance agents and issued by the American College in Bryn Mawr, Pennsylvania. The applicants must complete 10 college level courses and have three years field experience. After this they can take three more courses to obtain a Chartered Financial Consultant (CFC) certificate issued by the American College.
- ◆ Certified Public Accountant (CPA): Must pass rigorous tests administrated nationally and receive approval from their state accounting boards.
- ◆ Miscellaneous stock brokers, insurance agents, mutual fund agents, etc. All of these must obtain licenses that require specific courses and examinations.

INVESTMENTS

BANK ACCOUNTS:

Banks are in business to make money. Look around at the fancy buildings that are built with your money. The money you deposit is used by them to invest at a higher rate or to loan to others at a higher rate. Banks are necessary for our way of life. Use them to your benefit and know what you want to accomplish with the money you invest. Bank accounts are Federally insured up to $100,000.00 per account while most other investments are not.

With the changes in the law, many banks are now able to offer stock purchase, mutual funds, insurance policies, etc. Most of these accounts do not fall under the Federal insurance per-account. Check with your bank for the details before investing.

Banks charge fees for many of their services. See the chart at the end of this chapter and use it to compare the fees of your bank against two or three other banks, credit unions, etc. Consider these costs as well as your personal preference in dealing with the people involved. Look for a bank that is working for you and your interests. Be sure to assert yourself and get the best service.

> **HINT:** *Always balance your bank account monthly. Do not leave it up to your bank to do this.*

◆ Checking accounts are used for day to day expenses. In order to keep from incurring a monthly charge for usage, some banks require a minimum balance. A low interest rate is usually paid to you for the average monthly balance. Keeping a large amount of money in your checking account may

decrease your income if the interest is too low. Ask the bank about accounts for direct deposit, direct withdrawals, limited checking fees, etc.
- ◆ Savings accounts are a backup to checking accounts. They allow for emergencies. Some banks will transfer funds automatically from the savings to the checking when the checking account falls below the minimum. Check with your bank for details. Saving accounts pay more interest than a checking account, but interest is still low.
- ◆ Money market accounts pay more interest than savings accounts. They can be used as a backup for a checking account in conjunction with a savings account or as an alternative to having a separate savings account. Money in a money market account can be withdrawn without penalty. Some institutions allow check writing privileges with a minimum amount required for each check.
- ◆ Certificates of Deposit are better known as CD's. These certificates are purchased for a set amount of time at a set amount of interest. The interest is higher than the previous accounts but they cannot be withdrawn prior to the expiration date without a penalty. If this money will be needed before that date, it is not a wise investment. Different financial institutions offer different rates.

It is a good idea to shop around for the highest rate available. Most banks automatically roll over all CD's when they reach the expiration date. If you do not want this done, contact the bank and give specific written instructions as to what you want done at the expiration date.

MUTUAL FUNDS:

A mutual fund is a group of individual investors pooling their money under the supervision of a professional portfolio management team in an effort to gain profit. The fund buys and sells you shares of the mutual fund at the market value as of the close of the day they receive your order. The value of each share is determined by the current market value of all the stocks held by the mutual fund. Each mutual fund company, and there are thousands of them, furnishes a "prospectus" to give you information about the fund. This is required by law. This prospectus will give you the information you will need to make a rational decision. There are several reasons for investing in a mutual fund.

- ◆ **Liquidity:** Shares in a mutual fund may be redeemed at any time. Most funds will set the market value on the close of the day you notify them to liquidate all or part of your shares. Some funds offer loan benefits, transfers to another of their funds, or reinvestment benefits of the dividends and capital gains. Check your prospectus for the rules of each particular fund.
- ◆ **Diversification:** A mutual fund invests in many companies. The prospectus will tell you the type of investments as well a list of the companies. Instead of putting all your eggs in one basket (i.e., one stock), you will have a share in a variety of companies thereby minimizing your risks.
- ◆ **Management:** Professional fund managers have the facilities and the information needed to make investment decisions. They don't always pick the winners or avoid the losers, but they have the tools and the know-how to do the job.

- **Affordable:** A mutual fund lets you start an investment with a small amount of money. There are funds where you can start with a minimum of $50.00 or less. You can set up the account at your bank for an automatic monthly payment to invest and/or you can continue to invest with small amounts directly.

The costs vary in the purchase of a mutual fund. Salespeople work on commissions. Someone must pay them and of course, you being the buyer, will pay one way or the other. Each fund's prospectus will show the commissions, fees, and any other costs involved. The management fee is usually from ½ of 1% to 1% of the total amount invested. Some funds have what is known as a 12(b)1 cost that is a percentage of the fund's total assets deducted every year to cover marketing and the distribution expense. The business section of your paper will show the present market value per share of these funds.

- **No-load:** Some funds are what is known as no-load. Actually, you must read the fund's prospectus to find out the hidden charges and fees. Check the management fees, yearly costs, etc. Your whole investment goes to work instantly but, maybe, the costs over the long term may be higher.
- **Front-end loads:** In this type of mutual fund you pay the commission up front. That amount is then deducted from your investment and the balance of your money buys the shares. They may also have a low yearly fee. (This type of fund is desirable for a long term investment.)
- **Rear end load funds:** There is no commission on the original amount invested and may have a

yearly maintenance fee as well as a 12(b)1 fee. The commission is charged at withdrawal on the amount in the fund at that time. If you have reinvested dividends and/or the share price has gone up, you will pay a larger commission because the amount of the account is larger. Another way they have to recoup their sales fee is by a decreasing sales charge on the amount redeemed depending on the length of time invested.

Over the long term a front-end, no-load or any other fee is negligible. It takes about seven years in a fund to even out the fees involved.

> **Hint:** *Any changes you make involving financial transactions will have costs (fees) to them. Never believe there is a complete no-load and don't invest in something you don't understand.*

Mutual funds are set to specialize in different areas of investments. The fund you purchase must be what is good for you and should be based on your need for immediate income, future income, capital growth, or tax-free benefits. Each fund is formed or invested in areas with certain risk factors. It is very important to weigh the areas and the risk factors before you invest. Look for past performance. Look at the growth rate over a period of years. **Read the prospectus.**
- ◆ **Stock funds:**
    - a. Growth funds: Funds that are geared to long term capital growth and better than average returns.
    - b. Aggressive growth funds: Invest in smaller

companies with a great potential for growth. They can involve a greater risk for a greater possibility of growth.
   c. Income funds: Invest in private companies with a higher dividend rate (i.e., utility companies.) Growth potential is secondary to the dividend income.
   d. Equity income funds: Invest in companies that can be expected to gain growth along with income from regular dividends.
   e. Balanced funds: Invest in both stocks and bonds. Check out the prospectus for the amount and type of investments.

◆ **Bond funds:**
   a. Government funds: All fund money is invested in bonds backed by the United States Government. These investments might be bonds, treasury bills, treasury notes, or notes issued by specific agencies of the government (i.e., Ginnie Maes, Fannie Maes.)
   b. Corporate bond funds: There are two types:
      1. Quality funds investing in all high "quality" bonds issued by private corporations.
      2. High-Yield funds that invest in lower quality bonds with higher interest rates. (High-yield funds are often invested in junk bonds.)
   c. Tax-free funds: Invest in municipal bonds issued by municipal governments and special state funds issued by a specific state. These are tax free for Federal income taxes and tax free to the specific state income taxes. (Taxes, both Federal and state, will be due

INVESTMENTS

for any capital gains on the shares.)
- **Special funds:**
  a. Metals and natural resources: These can be oil, gas, gold etc. Remember, precious metals can be very volatile, so be sure to read the prospectus thoroughly.
  b. One sector funds: These funds are invested in only one field or specialty such as health, oil, tech stocks, etc. These can be very volatile, but can also be profitable.
  c. Foreign stock funds: These funds specialize in stock from only one country or from several countries. As the world changes the stocks held will be adjusted. If you are interested in this, read the information very carefully.

PORTFOLIO MANAGEMENT:

Go for diversifying, affordability, the ability to buy or sell easily, measure of safety and liquidity. There is no guarantee that you will make money. Use these guidelines in your basic or mutual fund planning:
- Review your financial situation.
- Choose only stocks, bonds or mutual funds that accomplish the goals you have set.
- Don't plan on taking money in and out of a fund — use it for long term investing.
- Be informed as to the type of equity or fund — read the prospectus and ask questions.
- In the long run, the investment is more important than the fee schedule.
- Invest regularly to cost average your investment.

- Reinvest dividends and capital gains when possible. (Great for retirement accounts.)
- Avoid high risk investments.
- Develop a plan to make the most of your assets and liabilities.

ANNUITIES:

A financial contract made with an insurance company for either deferred or immediate income. There are two kinds of annuities in which you can invest. The fixed rate annuities pay interest based on the prime rate and variable annuities based on the financial market. Read your policy carefully for type, redemption penalties etc. (See Chapter 7 "Retirement")

RETIREMENT ACCOUNTS:

Everyone, during their working years, should take part in a retirement plan. The main advantage, after knowing you will have retirement money, is the tax deferred advantage of a retirement plan. Not only will it defer the taxes on the initial investment amount, but it also will defer the taxes on any growth, interest or dividends reinvested in the plan. (See Chapter 7 "Retirement")

FEDERAL GOVERNMENT INVESTMENTS:
- Series EE bonds: (Issued by the United States Government)
    1. Credits interest twice a year and adds it to the total value upon redemption.
    2. Must hold a minimum of six months before interest is credited.
    3. To get the most interest, cash at the month

INVESTMENTS

you bought them or at six month intervals.
4. Check old bonds — they stop collecting interest after 40 years.
◆ U.S. Government Obligations: (Exempt from state and local taxes.)
1. Treasury Bills — issued for 6 and 12 months with the minimum investment of $10,000. Interest is the difference between what you pay and the maturity value of $10,000.
2. Treasury notes — mature in 2-10 years. Minimum investment for notes up to 4 years is $5,000, and longer notes are $1,000. Interest is paid twice a year.
3. Treasury bonds — usually have maturities of 30 years. Minimum purchase price is $1,000. Interest is paid twice a year.

REDUCE YOUR RISKS:
◆ Don't give authorization to make trades without your consent.
◆ Get a commission schedule and check on all fees charged — understand all terms before investing.
◆ Keep copies of all your paperwork.
◆ Ask for a prospectus for any proposed investment — ask questions if you don't understand.
◆ Note: The higher the return — the higher the risk.
◆ Don't rush into any decision or sign any documents without reading and understanding them.
◆ Check into the history of the firm that is handling your investments — call toll free to the National Association of Securities Dealers at 1-800-289-9999.

NOW ONE IS ALONE:

When you are alone, it is up to you to handle all the money, all the decisions, all the debt, and the future. Don't let grief, guilt or loneliness make the decisions for you. Some mistakes you will want to avoid are:

1. Avoid consoling yourself with excess and heat of the moment spending.
2. Avoid investing with the first person to contact you or too quickly without looking into their credentials.
3. Avoid letting family, friends or neighbors make up your mind for you.
4. Avoid immediate dependency on a family member or friend.
5. Avoid thinking, "I can't make a mistake." (You can and you will learn from this.)
6. Avoid letting emotions rule your money habits.

INVESTMENTS

Conparison Chart
(Copy this form.)

Checking

Financial Institution	Fees	Minimum Interest	ATM Costs

Savings

Financial Institution	Minimum Interest	CD Interest

Suddenly Alone

CHAPTER 5

∗

INSURANCE

INSURANCE

LIFE INSURANCE:

The term "life insurance" covers a labyrinth of needs. You might want insurance for college funds, mortgage protection, as an investment strategy, or maybe just as a death benefit to take care of the needs of your survivor. When you are shopping around for insurance, it is important to check your current needs as well as what your needs will be for the future.

The main purpose of life insurance is to provide future financial security for your family. It provides an immediate amount of money that will enable your family to maintain the household after you die. Life insurance is the basic tool for taking care of those who depend on you. Originally it was not designed to take care of your needs. Now with the changes in the insurance business and laws, there can be an advantage for you as well, but it takes planning and knowledge.

When you purchase a life insurance policy, you are buying into a risk-sharing group. Although no one can predict when any one will die, it is possible to accurately predict the number within a group category (i.e. nonsmoking men of a certain age) who will die within the next 50 years. The insurance industry calculates the premiums to reflect this risk and you are charged accordingly for the amount of benefits you purchase.

Fill in the form "Do I Need Life Insurance?" at the end of this chapter. This will give you a basis for need and you will be able to use it in your plan. Most insurance advisors suggest you have enough to cover your survivors' needs for up to five years. As an example, if it takes $35,000 a year to live at today's prices, you would need $175,000 in life insurance. Remember, this is a rule of thumb and your particular needs may be different. Also, you may be entitled to other benefits from other sources to make up some of the difference.

Take time to figure out what immediate financial funds will be needed in the case of your death. (See Chapter 13 "Estate Planning") Add to this the future obligations and all other commitments you want covered. If your survivors will have to relocate, they will need extra money. Also, include money for any health, education or other special problems. Add to this any other benefit you want them or yourself (investment benefit) to have.

From that figure subtract existing assets and benefits. This will give you a figure you need for death insurance.

TYPES OF INSURANCE:

Term insurance: It is exactly what the name implies. You pay a specific amount of money for a specific amount of insurance for a specific length of time. If you stop paying, the policy is canceled. If you die during that period of time, your beneficiaries get the insurance. If you live through the time, you get nothing. At different intervals of years the policy may be renewed but, the amount of the premium increases with age, while the amount of the insurance stays the same. Each time

the term is renewed the premium will rise. There are many benefits to this type of policy:
- ◆ The premiums are much lower than a whole life policy.
- ◆ You are able to reduce or increase the insurance depending on your needs.
- ◆ If you die, your beneficiary gets the full amount of insurance.
- ◆ You can have a much larger protection during the time your family is growing and the need is high.

Disadvantages include:
- ◆ If you stop paying, the policy is canceled.
- ◆ When the specific period of time ends, the policy has no value.
- ◆ There is no cash value or loan value built into the policy.

> **HINT:** *It is a good idea to buy term insurance with a "convertible" clause in case you want to convert to "whole life."*

PERMANENT INSURANCE:

Sometimes this has other names such as "whole life" or "universal life." It is insurance for life or until you stop paying the premium. This type of policy has a set amount of premium for life. There is also a set amount of insurance benefit for that period of time. Permanent insurance usually has an investment element built into the policy.

Consumer Report describes universal life insurance "like having two different policies at once — insurance and an investment account." It also means the buyer pays more in premiums in exchange for more benefits. Benefits can include a cash value, the ability to borrow against the policy, interest earnings, and tax deferral.

Advantages include:
- Nothing can cancel the insurance benefits unless you fail to pay the premiums. After a few years the policy usually has enough invested into it to give you short time extended coverage.
- The policy builds up a loan value with low interest rates.
- Cash value builds up and if you cancel the insurance you might get a refund of cash.

Disadvantages include:
- There is a higher premium for this type of insurance.
- This is a front load plan and unless you plan to hold it for an extended period of time, it is not to your advantage.
- It has an investment built into the policy that tends to be very expensive.

Before you purchase insurance, shop around for a good agent. There are agents out there interested in only the fast buck. Find one that is in it for the long haul and has your complete interest in mind. Check on the agent's reputation and credentials, who he does business with, and if he is active in the community. This is not a one time purchase. Your needs change and you want to be able to trust the agent you decide to do business with.

Basically, life insurance is to protect those you leave behind. When you purchase the insurance, you become the owner and as the owner you have certain rights. You have the right to name whomever you want as a beneficiary, you have the right to cancel the policy at any time, you have the right to any cash value, and you may have the right to borrow against the policy.

There is another way to handle this ownership and it is growing in popularity between married couples and between partners and executives in business. Ownership is put in the survivor's name. This allows the person that you want protected to control the policy. It transfers your right to name the beneficiary, your right to cancel the policy and any other benefit. It can also change to them the payment of the policy if you decide to suddenly stop paying.

> **Hint:** *If you want your survivor to have complete protection, you can change the policy ownership to his name.*

It is recommended that people evaluate their life insurance needs, buy from a company licensed in their state, select a trustworthy insurance agent, compare costs of similar policies and ask about lower rates for their group. **Finally, read your policy.** Know what is covered, what is not covered, and what benefits the policy contains. Obtain a copy of your application form and add it to your insurance records.

Life insurance is a must, even when you are single. Even single people die and when that happens, there are costs that must be paid. Life insurance is the best way for your survivors to be relieved of any possible financial burden:

◆ Last expenses — funeral, burial, obituaries, flowers, service, etc.
◆ Medical expenses.
◆ Legal fees — probate, administration, executor, etc.

Insurance

- ◆ Debt elimination — mortgage, credit cards, etc.
- ◆ Maintenance and distribution of assets.

As in all businesses, you must watch your agent and be informed. There are ways for insurance agents to make a lot more money than is necessary from your account. If at any time you believe that your best interests are not as important as his, or, if you believe something is wrong, write a letter to the manager or the company holding the insurance. Be sure you have evidence to prove your allegations. Companies tend to believe the agents, but with proof, they will listen to you.

When you receive your policy, check the original application to make sure nothing was changed. If the agent answered any questions for you, read the answers and make sure you agree with them. Check the policy for the coverage and be sure it covers what you agreed to purchase. Make sure every page is there and the pages are in consecutive order. Finally, write to the customer-relations office of the insurance company and get a copy of the "agent's report" that accompanied your application. Check this report to make sure it is all true and no false claims were made to the company.

There are certain sales deceptions to watch for:
- ◆ Churning — any replacement will give the agent another commission. Be informed and decide if a new policy is right for you.
- ◆ Premiums — your agent told you that you would only be paying premiums for a fixed number of years, then the policy was paid for. The years are up but, the premiums go on.
- ◆ Piggybacking — offer of another policy at a reduced or free premium. It can use the value, the dividends and loans for the other policy to pay

the premium. Eventually the other policy will lapse or just run out of cash.
◆ Investment — the policy is sold to use as an investment as well as life insurance. You might have been told this is for college, retirement etc. and was a tax-free investment. You then found it was just ordinary life insurance.

> **HINT:** *Get full disclosure from your agent and then read the policy carefully. Ask questions if you do not understand the terms.*

SECOND TO DIE INSURANCE:

A type of life insurance that is used to provide enough money to cover your future estate taxes. It is primarily an estate planning instrument that pays only after the death of the insured that lives the longest. This insurance is purchased when it is necessary for the children to have money when both parents die to pay for the taxes and any other expenses that have been postponed after the death of the first parent because of the marital estate deduction.

OTHER PERSONAL INSURANCE:

After you have worked out what your immediate needs might be, it is time to work on the other goals you might have. Disability insurance should come high on your list. What happens if you are disabled tomorrow and your income stops? Do you need mortgage insurance to cover the full amount of your mortgage? Does the mortgage insurance remain a specific amount or does it decrease as the mortgage is paid off? Do you need insurance such as an "annuity" for investment and tax deferral?

Cigma Property and Casualty of Philadelphia started offering a policy in August of 1996 aimed at people paying child support and for people that are in danger of losing their jobs because of corporate downsizing. The policy does not cover you if you quit the job.

HOMEOWNER'S INSURANCE:

The goal for your homeowner's policy is to buy exactly what you need at the lowest price. Many people never read the policy and then when something happens, they find they are not covered. The necessary things you must know are, the limits of coverage, how much the deductible is and what disaster coverage is included.

Let's talk about the basic mechanics of your policy:
- Property protection — This includes the coverage against what the insurance companies call "named perils." It could be fire, smoke damage, hail, tornadoes, explosions, riots, theft, vandalism, and falling aircraft.
- Liability protection — This is coverage in the event that you accidentally hurt someone or damage their property. It can include medical treatment, costs to restore or repair their property and legal costs if you or a family member is responsible.

Long ago my father told me, "The small things that happen to you, you can handle. Insure yourself for disasters than can destroy you financially." He was right. If the back window and frame are broken, it is small compared to what it would cost if a tree fell through the roof or if someone broke a hip on the stairs. With that in mind, how much coverage do you need?

Decide what perils are on your current policy and how much it will pay in dollar amounts. You want it to be equal to or close to what it might cost you to rebuild your home. (Replacement cost.) It's only the amount to rebuild, not the cost of the land. Most insurers will not sell you a policy with less than 80 percent coverage. It is wise not to go below this limit.

For complete protection, you should consider "guaranteed replacement cost" coverage. This will be more expensive but, if your home is destroyed by any of the perils listed in your policy, you will receive the full cost to replace it.

Any personal property coverage will also be listed in the policy. This is only for your personal belongings and is a separate amount from the coverage on the actual home. Check the amount to make sure it is adequate. Also check to make sure the coverage on jewelry, collections, computers, home business equipment, etc. is adequate. Some policies do not cover these items.

Liability protection listed on your policy covers you for others' property damage and/or injury caused by you, your pets and family members living with you. Does your policy offer you enough protection? How much is enough? The normal coverage is about $100,000. For a major occurrence, this isn't very much. As jury awards in negligence suits skyrocket, carrying ample insurance has become critical.

Check into an umbrella policy. Umbrella policies cover you for the extra liability protection that is over and above the limits on your homeowner's policy. It can add more protection on other perils not covered on

INSURANCE

your policy such as slander, invasion of privacy, etc. To decide how much extra protection you need, consider what you have to lose. You need to be covered in case of a catastrophic event to protect assets and savings.

Saving ideas to lower your homeowner's policy costs:
- Increase the deductible.
- Insure only the building and not the extra for the land.
- Install smoke alarms, burglar alarms or deadbolt locks.
- Be a nonsmoker.
- Check into senior discounts.
- Upgrade your policy once a year to eliminate coverage not needed.
- Upgrade your roof, electrical, plumbing, etc.

> **HINT:** *Be aware of your insurance policy's exclusions. Buy supplemental insurance where necessary.*

RENTER'S POLICY:
You are not a homeowner but, you still need insurance for your personal property and belongings. There are policies that will cover you in case these are damaged, destroyed or even stolen. Some policies cover temporary living expenses if you are forced out of your rental home. Check for a replacement-cost policy and an umbrella policy to cover all your needs.

AUTOMOBILE INSURANCE:

Each type of insurance requires a different agent's license in your state. In the case of auto insurance, it is even more important to deal with someone you trust and a company with a long standing reputation. For this, I am going to break the policy down into parts so you will understand what is covered.

> **HINT:** *Each policy has a limit of liability that the company will pay. Read your policy and make sure it has enough coverage to protect you.*

Liability coverage: Each state has its own requirements as to the amount you must carry. Check with your state insurance commissioner for the amounts.

- ◆ Property damage — Damage to someone else's property from an automobile accident when you are a covered driver and are legally responsible. This is damage to someone else's property, not yours.
- ◆ Bodily injury — If you are the covered driver on your policy and you are legally liable in the automobile accident in which others are injured or killed, the insurance will cover those in the other automobile. This is for persons directly hurt from an automobile accident, not to you.

No-fault coverage: Check with your state as to the requirements.
- ◆ In some states you must sign off if you don't want to be covered under no-fault.
- ◆ Covers the other party involving a legally liable uninsured or under insured driver.

Insurance

- ◆ Coverage for you, your family and your passengers — injury, death, loss of income, etc.

Medical coverage:
- ◆ For you, your family, and your passengers.
- ◆ Usually a small amount. Check this carefully.

Collision coverage:
- ◆ For your automobile damage in an accident.
- ◆ Usually has a deductible. (You pay a higher premium for a lower deductible.)

Comprehensive coverage:
- ◆ Damage from falling objects, weather, fire, theft, vandalism, etc.
- ◆ Usually has a deductible. (You pay a higher premium for a lower deductible.)

Remember if you have assets to lose, you will want a higher amount of liability. The insurance company is limited as to the amount they must pay. You are not limited and if you are found liable for more damage than the insurance company pays, it will have to come out of your pocket. Rates for automobile insurance vary greatly. Be sure to ask your agent for all discounts:

- ◆ Two-car families. (Or even three and four cars.)
- ◆ Drivers who have taken "drivers' ed" courses.
- ◆ Over 55 years old discount.
- ◆ Experience and/or safe drivers.
- ◆ Increased deductible amounts.
- ◆ Use of one insurer for all insurance.

Do You Need Life Insurance?
(Make a copy)

NEEDS
    IMMEDIATE EXPENSES:
        Funeral costs $_____
        Medical bills   _____
        Property maintenance   _____
        Probate costs   _____
        Legal fees   _____
        Federal estate taxes   _____
        State estate taxes   _____
            Total $_____

    FUTURE EXPENSES:
        Family expense account $_____
        Emergency fund   _____
        Child-care expenses   _____
        Mortgage   _____
        Debts   _____
        College & education   _____
            Total $_____
    Total needs $_____

ASSETS
        Cash and savings $_____
        Equity in home   _____
        Other real estate equity   _____
        Securities   _____
        Retirement accounts   _____
        Employer savings plans   _____
        Lump sum pension benefit   _____
        Life insurance cash value   _____
        Current life insurance   _____
        Other assets   _____
    Total assets $_____

EXTRA INSURANCE NEEDED
    Total needs $_____
    Minus total assets   _____
        Additional insurance needed $_____

CHAPTER 6

✷

MEMORIES

MEMORIES

Pedigree charts are only the names and dates of your ancestors. Give those that follow you more. You have important history and now is the time to start preserving all the family memories you carry around in your head. Try to do this between the two of you. Once you are alone one half of the memories are gone. Don't let the other half get away. Start recording your thoughts, your life and your memories. Begin — close your eyes and picture your parents or grandparents. Think about your first memory of them and why that memory is important. From that point, these hints will help you:

- ◆ How much can you remember about your family history before you were born? Did your parents or grandparents tell you stories about their lives? Jot down what you remember in a notebook or a tape. Add to it as you remember more. Let it grow. It will come to life for you. Describe these people and the times and clothes they wore. Draw pictures of them or add a photograph. What were their personalities, occupations, special skills, education, physical appearance, health etc.
- ◆ Where were you born? Tell what the area was like, the first home you lived in or remember. What did you like to do? Talk about your school, friends you had, the hobbies, activities or sports you enjoyed.

MEMORIES

- Were there trips to other countries to check into ancestry or traditions?
- Did your family celebrate holidays? What special traditions were important to you? (Birthdays, Christmas, Halloween.)
- Were there any special relationships you had with your brother or sister, maybe a cousin?
- Do you have any memories of the depression? Did your family tell you about their experiences during that time? Were you wealthy or poor? What are you now? Give examples if you can.
- What about special activities with your parents? (Camping, hiking, cooking, woodworking.) Which of these were most important for shaping your life?
- As a child, what were you like? Were you outgoing, quiet, a loner, needing to be with others or content to just go with the flow of the moment? Did you feel you were popular, conceited, pretty, handsome etc? Were you creative, did you like to paint, read or let your imagination take hold of you? What made you different from your brothers and sisters?
- Tell about the happy times of your life as well as the sad times. What was the most happy and what was the most sad?
- List health problems you have had. Do you think any of them could be hereditary? What about your health now? Are there any health problems your parents or grandparents may have had that should be listed for future generations?
- Tell about your first love. What was so special about that first love? Is that the person you are with now? Do you remember your first kiss? Bring

to life the courtship and marriage and the wedding. How did you meet? Was it a small or a large wedding? Do you still have any wedding gifts? Who were they from and who do you want to have them after you are gone?
- ◆ Tell about your work. If you haven't worked tell about your activities that are of most interest to you. Tell about your spouse's work or visa versa.
- ◆ Detail the raising of your children. (Special times, problems, descriptions, activities, etc.) What were they like as babies, as small children, as teens and as young adults? How did it feel to hold them in your arms at different times?
- ◆ Who were the heros of your life? Relate how some people influenced you and the results. Who was the one person that you remember most vividly and why?
- ◆ What were the turning points of your life? When were these turning points and how did you cope with them? Which one was the most important and the results?
- ◆ Finish with how you feel about life, your beliefs, your faith and what you want for the future of your family. What advice do you want to give your children, your grandchildren and future generations? Give them your legacy to know you and love you.

As you can see there is more to memories than birthdays and special dates. As an example, I will tell you one of the stories I wrote for my grandchildren. Enjoy it, get some ideas from it and start sharing your stories.

SATURDAY LIVE
By Catherine Wannamaker

It's Saturday. I've finished putting my toys away. It's Saturday and the weather is cold and crisp, there's snow on the ground, . . . but I don't care. It's Saturday and I'm going to the movies.

My growing up years were during the growing, golden era of films. There are gun shooting westerns with cowboys and scalp hunting Indians. There are films full of horrors and monsters. It is the time of the musical extravaganza, "Ziegfield Follies". There are cartoons, cliff hanger serials of cowboys and science fiction.

Within walking distance of home were two show houses. The first one is only about nine blocks away. It doesn't have my favorite serial though. My brother and sister and I would much rather walk the extra six blocks to the Paradise, down near the point of National and Greenfield. The Paradise shows several cartoons, a double feature and sometimes they even have contests during intermission.

Mom gave us each a dime for the show and we are carrying a sack of goodies. She knows we get hungry and need something to nibble on. She probably put in a sandwich too. Dad is pretty special. Today, he gave me an extra nickel for popcorn. I hold it tight in my hand as we walk quickly. We don't want to be late.

The front of the show house is all lit up. The posters on the wall show the coming features. Look, "King Kong" is coming again. He is invincible as he sits on the top of the Empire State Building swatting at the airplanes. Look at those posters. "Flash Gordon Conquers the Universe" and a Buck Roger's serial is coming. I must come to see every episode.

The man at the ticket window looks at us to make sure we

are under twelve. We give him our dimes and he sells us each a ticket. I walk in and walk right by the popcorn stand. Even the tantalizing smell of freshly popped corn doesn't tempt me. It's still too early to spend my nickel. Besides, I want to get in and get the best seat. Hand in hand we slither through the crowd and right up to the front row. We grab 3 seats and stake out our claim for the afternoon. Behind us the seats start to fill. The kids are yelling and laughing. I see some of my friends. They, too, are excited and waiting to see —what has become of our hero.

The room darkens and the screen comes to life. A Disney cartoon, "The Tortoise and the Hare" begins. Always . . . we get to see 2 cartoons and maybe even 3 or 4. Sometimes there are other short subjects or a newsreel.

The short subject is a two reel "Our Gang Comedy." I could be part of that gang. I follow their movements and dialogue. The little fat boy, Spanky, always rushing to catch up. And Alfalfa, I can picture him in my mind. He is a tall skinny kid with a cowlick in his hair that stands straight up and a face covered with freckles. He was the leader and led them through adventure after adventure. There was one little girl, Rosemary. She was the only girl in "Our Gang Comedies" and we all envied her. We followed their antics and their troubles. We laughed with them, fantasized with them and even cried with them. Yes, today is a very special Saturday.

Then the first feature fills up the screen. It is a thriller of gangsters and prohibition staring Walter Houston, Jean Hersholt and Edward Arnold. I only wish it were in Technicolor. The good guys versus the bad guys! The shoot-em-ups! We sit on the edge of our seats to catch every word.

The lights come on. It's intermission time. Everyone is talking and moving around. A piece of paper flies by my head. Now is the time to run out and get popcorn. Maybe I won't get popcorn. Maybe I'll get some candy or Crackerjack instead. This was a decision I had thought about all week and still haven't made up my mind. Finally the popcorn wins and I rush to take it back to my seat. I don't want to miss a minute of intermission.

It already has taken too long to get my popcorn and my brother is up on the stage. He entered the contest this week. He is up there with the others showing their "Yo Yo" skills. John works it up and down, over and under. He tries hard, but the big boy at the end of the line wins. He always wins!

The room darkens again and the previews come on. Even these we watch with rapt attention. We all want to know what is coming. Soon there would be Shirley Temple in "Little Miss Marker." She is a favorite and we will be coming to see it, even Mon and Dad. Tuesday is the day we come to the movies. That's the day they give away dishes. Mom is collecting the pretty green and pale pink plates. These dishes are now called depression glass and I still have a few.

Next week will be a Swashbuckler movie. Errol Flynn in "Captain Blood." It's the good guy against the bad guys swinging and fighting with swords instead of guns. The second feature is a Laurel and Hardy's called "Pack Up Your Troubles." I've seen it before, but it doesn't matter.

The previews are over. Anticipation is building. Now is the time. We waited all week to see what happened. The serial is about to begin. Is my hero alive or lying somewhere wounded or captured? When the episode ended last week, the bank robber was shooting directly at him and he jumped off the roof. How could he possibly protect himself from a fall to the hard ground? Did any of the bullets hit him? What about the rest of the gang that was waiting in the street below? How could he get away from them? Where was his trusted horse? Was he dead? All week we worried and pondered his fate.

Suddenly Alone

The audience is quiet. There is no sound except the quick intake of breath. The serial begins. The robber is shooting at the hero. He goes over the roof and grabs a window ledge as he is falling. There is a close-up of determination on his face. And then he swings himself through the glass window and runs down the hall and out the back way. He gives a loud whistle and his trusty steed comes running. He leaps into the saddle and away he goes to safety only to have the bandits follow. The new adventure begins. **But***, suddenly as my hero is about to save the fair maiden from the robbers, the killer shows up. They fight. The killer captures the hero and lashes him to the railroad tracks. I can hear the train in the distance. I grip the arms of my seat and — the screen goes blank. Finally the inevitable words come across the screen "continued next week."*

The main feature comes on. There is a strange quiet as the audience settles down. Doctor Frankenstein is robbing graves and taking body parts to his lab. I can see him putting the parts and pieces together and building a huge monster. I slide down in my seat and cover my eyes. The monster is laying on this cold table. Built into his shoulders are two posts. They are hooked up to the power machine. I shiver and slide farther down. Peeking trough my fingers, I see the Doctor throw the power switch. The monster twitches and slowly rises off the table. He walks.

The movies! Saturdays are a day for imagination and entertainment. Saturdays are for cowboys and pirates, songs and dance, good guys and bad guys, monsters and horrors. Saturdays are for Edward G. Robinson and Will Rogers, for Lionel Barrymore and Greta Garbo, for Douglas Fairbanks and Clark Gable, for Wallace Berry and Joan Crawford.

Movies took me through places and experiences I never thought possible. Movies influenced my opinions, my val-

ues, and maybe even my actions. Movies are a branch of my social history.

I remember those days of the movies and how much I wanted to be a star. I copied the Shirley Temple style. I walked around like Judy Garland. And then the first full feature Disney animated cartoon came out and I knew I would marry the prince just like Snow White. And maybe . . .

TO BE CONTINUED NEXT WEEK

Suddenly Alone

CHAPTER 7

*

RETIREMENT

RETIREMENT

RETIREMENT ACCOUNTS

Everyone, during their working years, should take part in a retirement plan either through their employer or individually. The main advantage, after knowing you will have retirement money, is the tax-deferred preference of a retirement plan. It not only will defer the taxes on the initial investment amount, but will defer the taxes on growth, interest or dividends reinvested in the plan.

HOW MUCH WILL YOU NEED FOR RETIREMENT?

Usually you will need between 60% and 100% of your current income to live comfortably in retirement. The percentage varies depending on your current situation. Some of the expenses will change and you should use Form #2 in the Financial Statement chapter to adjust these. Some of the changes will be in savings, children, education, taxes, etc. If at all possible, you should work to have all debts paid before retirement.

Once you determine your comfortable monthly income for retirement in current dollars, the future value of this amount can be found. Find the closest five-year interval between now and your planned retirement date on the next page, multiply your present value by the decimal number associated with the five-year interval: the result is about what you'll need per month when you retired. This is based on a cost of living increases of 3.25% per year.

Future Value Multipliers

Years to Retirement	Multiplier
Five years	1.173
10 years	1.377
15 years	1.616
20 years	1.896
25 years	2.225
30 years	2.610
35 years	3.063

Example: If in today's dollars, you will need $1,800 per month to live comfortably when you retire. You plan to retire in 20 years. The calculation is: $1,800 x 1.896 = $3,413 per month in 20 years.

WHAT WILL BE THE SOURCES OF RETIREMENT INCOME?

For most individuals, there are four basic retirement income sources: Social Security, pensions, employer tax-deferred savings plans and personal investments. (IRAs, investments and personal savings.)

Retirement accounts are built with time for growth and time limits on withdrawals. The normal age for withdrawal is 59½, but as with all other tax regulations there are many exceptions. New legislation is always being passed and requirements changing. Check with your tax accountant or the IRS for information. Money drawn from any retirement account is taxable. If it is drawn out prior to age 59 ½, there will also be a penalty of 10%, unless it qualifies for one of the exceptions.

- ◆ 401(k) are plans invested through your employer with a percentage from your earned income and a set percentage contributed by the employer. Each year the employer will give you a statement of gains and losses. Check each statement to be sure the amount invested is correct as well as the amount credited by the employer. Keep all statements and a copy of each W-2 until retirement. Companies are known to lose information as unions change and companies change ownership.
- ◆ IRA's (Individual Retirement Accounts) are contributions made into an individual investment plan and deducted on the individual's income tax. There is a limit of $2,000 per person or the amount of income if less. Starting in 1997 an amount of $2,000 may be invested into an IRA for a non-working spouse.

IRA plans remain in the name of one person. Your account should list a beneficiary and possibly an alternate beneficiary. Keep these current or at your death, the money will be put into the estate and the entire amount taxed in one lump.

You must begin to withdraw from your plan when you reach the age of 70 ½. The withdrawal will have a minimum amount based on life expectancy tables. You can, however, draw more than that each year. Unlike insurance annuities and other plans, IRA's have flexible amounts and you

Retirement

have the control over deposits and withdrawals.

At your death there are options available to the beneficiary. A spouse is able to roll it to one in his own name to avoid paying tax until a later date. If it is rolled over, the same age and life expectancy requirements will be required. (Check with IRS Publication 590 for further information.)

Example: Ten years ago, I persuaded a friend of mine to start an IRA retirement plan. She had just been divorced and was starting life on her own. Luckily, she was to receive alimony for the next several years. (Alimony is considered earned income and eligible for an IRA tax deduction.)

She opened her retirement plan with an initial payment of $1,000 to cover the first half of the current year. After that she authorized a direct withdrawal from her checking account and had it sent directly to the IRA plan. Over the years, she watched it grow. She watched the stock market go up and down and her shares in the plan went up and down. But, steadily the value of each share went up and the account grew and grew.

Now nine years have passed and she continues to invest. To date she has invested $18,000, a little at a time. Her account value is over $38,000 and she has another 12 years before retirement at age 65. Her account can double, triple, and even more if she continues to invest. Her words to me the other day were, "If you hadn't made me do this, I would have spent the money and had nothing."

A Roth IRA has been included in the law to be effective starting in 1998. This new type of IRA will not give you a tax deduction up front, but will let all the money taken out after a 5 year period be tax-free. You cannot take it out before age 59½, but unlike the traditional IRA, money can be put in after age 70½ and you are not required to make any withdrawals for as long as you live. Check with you tax accountant or financial advisor.

◆ Tax-sheltered annuities may be available for employees of tax-exempt organizations such as schools and hospitals. Distribution from these are listed later in this chapter. Check with your employer for a booklet that will give information on deposits, withdrawal, survivor benefits, etc.

◆ Deferred compensation plans are sometimes available for employees of state and local governments. Many corporations are using deferred compensation plans for their top officers.

◆ Miscellaneous plans — Self-Employed Plan (SEB), Thrift Savings plans, etc. — check with the IRS, your tax accountant or your financial advisor about any that can affect you.

> **HINT:** *Keep beneficiaries current on any retirement plan. If you don't, the money will go to your estate and require probate.*

Retirement plans are paid to your estate if you do not list a beneficiary. If it is paid to the estate, the full amount is immediately taxable. (Both for income taxes and estate taxes.) If a beneficiary is named and is still living, there can be other taxable deferred options and rollovers available. A problem will develop if the beneficiary is no longer living. **Keep the retirement account and the beneficiary current.**

ANNUITIES:

A financial contract made with an insurance company for either deferred or immediate income is called an annuity. A deferred annuity contract is an approved IRS plan and is part of a retirement plan offered by schools or state governments. All monies invested in these have not had the income taxes paid and the taxes will be paid upon withdrawal.

Regular annuities bought directly through an insurance company are bought with monies where income tax has already been paid. The income from these annuities, left in as reinvested, will be reinvested tax free. Then as the money is withdrawn at the annuity starting date, a certain percentage of each withdrawal will be taxable. (The principle is withdrawn tax-free and the earnings are taxable.)

There are two types of annuities you can invest in: (See IRS Publication 575 for further information.)

- ◆ Fixed rate annuities pay interest adjusted annually to market rates. Your returns will fluctuate Fixed annuities are considered a safe investment much like a CD. And, just as in a CD investment, there is a penalty for early withdrawal. The interest is based on the insurance companies interest schedule.
- ◆ Variable annuities are subject to market risks. You can lose money or you can make money, depending on the equity market. You can lose earnings and even principal. Read your policy carefully and know what you are investing in and what the redemption penalties might be.

> *HINT: Expenses vary greatly with insurance companies. Shop around for the best policy for you and be sure to check any continuing fees. Withdrawal charges vary with the different policies.*

For a free copy of *Life Advice: About Annuities*, write to Consumer Information Center, Dept. 58, Pueblo, Colorado 81009.

Benefits from annuities are paid in several different ways. Be sure to check which type of payment will best suit your needs. Once you have made a choice, you cannot change to another plan. Consider payment for a $100,000 annuity:

- ◆ Fixed period — A defined amount will be received for a definite period of time. Example, you choose this option to be paid for a period of 15 years the amount of $500 per month. If you live only seven years, you will receive $90,000. The balance of $10,000 will go to your beneficiary. If you live nineteen years, the payments will have stopped after the fifteenth year leaving you without the income.
- ◆ Payment over your lifetime — The insurance company will figure this amount based on their life expectancy tables. You will receive this amount for the rest of your life, no matter how long that tends to be. If the figure was $500 per month and if you die after 15 years, you will receive $90,000. The balance of $10,000 will go to the insurance company and your survivors will get nothing.
- ◆ Payment for yours and a survivor's lifetime — Again this is figured on the life expectancy tables.

RETIREMENT

The first annuitant receives a definite amount at regular intervals for life. After his death, the second annuitant receives a definite amount at regular intervals for their lifetime. This is a lower figure, but the survivor receives an income for life.

◆ Variable payments — Payments that may vary in amounts for a definite length of time or for life depend on the option chosen. The variables might include profits from the investment or cost of living. Check with the insurance company about this.

SOCIAL SECURITY:

All benefits through the Social Security system are governed by Federal law. During your working years you make payments that are taken directly from your pay or as a self-employed person through estimate payments. The amount of your future benefit then builds with the number of years working. Form SSA-7004-PC-OPI is available from the Social Security Administration. It allows you to request an earnings and benefit estimate statement. Call your local office or write to:

Social Security Administration
Wilkes-Barre Data Operations Center
P.O. Box 20
Wilkes-Barre, PA 19703

Social Security is like an insurance plan for your future. You are a participant and are covered for several specific possibilities:

◆ Disability — You should file a claim as soon as you can after becoming disabled and benefits can begins after a five month waiting period. The waiting period begins with the month Social Security decides your disability started. You must have

worked the last five years under the Social Security system to qualify. As with any other government regulation there are exceptions to this basic rule. Check with the Social Security office if you have a question.
- ◆ Retirement benefits — A reduced rate is available at age 62 with the benefits' increasing if you start drawing benefits after age 62. Check with your local office on the graduating scale for retirement.
- ◆ Spousal benefits — A spouse will get a percentage of your Social Security and can begin at age 62 if you are drawing benefits.
- ◆ Widow(er) benefits — A widow(er) can begin receiving benefits at age 60.
- ◆ Divorce spouses — In order to qualify after being divorced, you must have been married a minimum of 10 years. The same rules then will apply to you as long as you are divorced. This is true even if you were married again and divorced.
- ◆ Minor children — Children of a deceased-qualified person can receive benefits as long as they are under age 18, or age 19 if still in high school. If you remarry, this will not affect their benefits.
- ◆ Burial allowance — The current burial allowance is $250 to be paid to a qualified survivor.
- ◆ Supplemental Social Security — (called SSI) It pays monthly checks to individuals who are 65 or older, blind, or disabled that do not have a lot of income or assets.

To apply for any benefit through the Social Security Administration you should take with you the following documentation:

- Your Social Security Card (also the Social Security Card of the deceased if needed).
- Your Birth Certificate (also the Birth Certificate of the deceased if needed).
- Children's Birth Certificates (if they are applying).
- Marriage Certificate (if applying on a spouse's record).
- Your most recent W-2 or tax return.
- Military Discharge papers if you or your spouse had military service.

PENSIONS:

A pension is generally a series of payments made after retirement from work. Pensions are made regularly for past service by an employer. This may include a company, the Federal or state government, an organization or a military pension.

There are different items to consider when you retire. The pension can usually be taken out with a single pension recipient or a portion of it can be deducted to provide the spouse a pension for life. Federal law states that a spouse must sign off on the pension if full benefits are chosen rather than when survivor benefits are chosen. Ask yourself if the pension holder dies:

- Does the pension die or does the survivor receive the benefits?
- Can your spouse survive if there isn't a provision for the pension to continue after your lifetime?
- When you start to receive Social Security, will there be an offset of part of the pension?
- Will pension benefits be paid out in one lump sum?

Keep monitoring your pension plan even after retirement. Companies tend to make changes and you must be aware of these. Make sure your pension account is current and has the correct address, beneficiary, tax deductions and exemptions. Keep a copy of your pension plan, a summary of each year's report, how many hours and days accumulated and the amount already paid to you.

> **HINT:** *Find out your options and do what is best for the long term rather than the short term.*

VA BENEFITS:

Benefits received from the Veterans Administration are for the person receiving them. Sometimes there are benefits for spouses, but you must apply for them. Also, your spouse may have VA life insurance. Check with the VA if you have any questions. Keep current all beneficiaries and addresses.

> **ONE FINAL NOTE:**
> Every retirement plan is set up differently. Locate the booklet or papers that describes alternate payouts and benefits. If this is not available, call the plan holder and request a copy of the information. Your attorney can obtain this in the settlement of an estate but, like everything else, it will cost you money to let him do it. **It is important for you to know all the benefits available.** Be informed!

CHAPTER 8

✳

RETIREMENT STORY

WHEN ONE IS ALONE

WHEN ONE IS ALONE

There is more to planning than just financial. This story is one idea toward planning for retirement and whatever happens. It's just a story, but then all stories have truth built into them.

Your mind is a computer, except you can think, reason and apply your conclusions. Don't let it go to waste. Use it, plan with it, make it work for you.

We've all moved to Florida. Maybe the move was brought about by business, maybe by family, or maybe by plans to retire in the sunshine far away from the snow and cold of winter. Whatever the reason, we all are here to make a better, happier, and more fruitful way of life. I would like to acquaint you with one idea that was offered to me and many others. Let me tell you about my friend.

Bill and Jean moved here several years ago. Bill was a salesman up north in the eastern part of the country. He traveled most of the time and left Jean on her own during the week. She had her own activities and friends she had made over the years. Bill had his business friends he saw during the week. It was a busy and hectic time and they valued their few evenings at home in peace and quiet. They had weekend friends. They partied with them and maybe enjoyed a game of bridge in the evening. And through it all the children were close and stopped by often. It was a good life and they both felt very secure. Now the lure of retirement reared and the

Retirement — When One Is Alone

two of them made the decision to leave the ice and snow and buy a lovely home in Florida.

What did they do to bridge the gap between the fast paced life of the work, children, separate activities, and leaving friends to a strange new environment and leisure? It was a big step for them to take, but luckily they had given it a lot of thought during the few years before retirement. Jean knew it would be difficult to have more husband around the house. She was used to her freedom during the day and sometimes nights. Now he would not be going to work. What would he do? What would she do?

They both knew that too much togetherness might cause some tension, so both set about to learn other skills. The skill I am impressed with is how they improved their bridge game. Bridge is a game of skill and cunning, a game of friends and interests, a game of competition or quiet enjoyment, a game of memory and constant awareness. Doesn't that sound like the whole way of life to most of us? I think so.

I'd like to look at the advantages of knowing how to communicate and play this fancy and ever-changing pastime that is called **BRIDGE**. It sharpens your mind and keeps you alert. Where else can you enjoy making so many decisions in so short a time? In each hand there are 13 cards. The first decision is to bid at each of your turns. If the decisions are right, then you and your partner will come to the best contract. If they are wrong, you're in a heap of trouble. Major decision? Yes! Fun? Yes! Life shaking? No! Then, with these 13 cards there are 13 times to make more right or wrong choices. Which card was played? Why? Do I finesse? If I do this, what will the opponents do? Decisions — Decisions!!

Bridge sharpens your memory and keeps you alert. During the course of the play of each game there are 52 cards to be remembered in sequence, maybe; already played, certainly;

possibility of who has what, essential; and of course which one to play at what time. The mind automatically becomes the computer as it keeps each and every card and its location in place. The best thing about all of this is that the alternative choices are weighed and reasoned unconsciously. All the memory courses in the world cannot achieve this relaxed method that is always going on as you learn and improve.

As Bill and Jean found, it was an advantage. They found new friends with the same interests. It was a means to get them out to bridge clubs. It was a means of communication to break the gap to new friends. It was a way to help make togetherness have some extra advantages. It was also a boon to the finding of friends individually. Examples of this could be: The Newcomers Club, Fraternal organizations, a local duplicate group and, of course, the wonderful neighbors we all have. I would always advise each and every person to take up bridge to help bridge the gap to new friends and activities.

Maybe the most important point in all of this comes when a person suddenly becomes one instead of two in the home. No matter what the reason, a person is suddenly alone. With today's social structure such, aloneness is suddenly a whole new world. More so than the changing from work to retirement. Now you have gone from togetherness and togetherness friends to alone with probably very few alone friends.

How do you start all over? It's easy to become a hermit. Many people, both men and women, do. That will just let the mind and body fall apart and make you a dull and lifeless individual. It is necessary sometimes to force yourself to take the initiative and get up and out on your own. Bridge and other courses are offered by community colleges, vocational schools, park systems and other places to get you into the game of bridge. New comradeship can be found. New avenues can be opened. You just have to get off your duff and do it!

Retirement — When One Is Alone

*Bridge is played at many levels. The first level is the learner or beginner. A friendly, and I stress it should always be a **friendly** game, can be found. Your game will develop with experience and you will find the level where you are comfortable. Maybe it's a game with friends, a game with companionship, a game of wits, or the challenge of a tournament.*

If that seems dull to some of you, the next step can be a duplicate game. In this town it is possible to play practically every afternoon and every evening. I think there are also a few morning games. You don't need a partner. A call to any of the groups will find you a partner. There is no reason whatsoever to say, "I don't know anyone." Even the duplicate game can put you in at your skill level to give you a chance to compete. Duplicate is the name used for competition with other bridge players. It opens up new avenues to test the memory and mind. Your computer mind must continually be used and updated or it becomes lifeless and obsolete.

If a person wants to go a step further then there is tournament bridge. Again a game is easy to find and it is easy to find a partner. There are sectional tournaments, regional tournaments, national tournaments and international tournaments. Where would you like to play? How about a tournament right here in town. Or, maybe one of the national tournaments in San Francisco over Thanksgiving. They are wonderful and the people participating are tremendous. I know because I have been to them.

Well, Bill and Jean found new friends. Their life found richness and happiness in our town. Their plans to retire and find fresh and new interests were fulfilled. Now that one of them is alone, there is still the reason to get up and out.

That Regional tournament is at the Hyatt this afternoon. I only need two red points to make Life Master. Maybe today I'll win these. He'd like that.

Suddenly Alone

CHAPTER 9

*

LOANS

LOANS

Taking out a loan or borrowing from a friend is not to be taken lightly. There are right reasons and there are wrong reasons to put yourself in debt. Either way, the bills must be paid and you will be completely responsible. Look through this section, read every word and analyze your reasons and what is the best for you.

RIGHT REASONS:
- Major purchases including items such as a home, an automobile or even education for yourself or your family. These are long term commitments and you must go into them with your eyes wide open. Don't go into them if it will put a financial strain on your budget. They are like the Energizer Bunny, they go on and on and on . . .
- Emergencies are the second main reason for you to borrow. Medical expenses, loss of employment as well as many unforseen problems can develop. Emergencies can overwhelm your cash reserve and a loan may be the only solution.
- Protecting your cash reserve is important. Credit purchases for a major appliance, a boat or possibly that new computer may be preferable. This can keep you from destroying the nest egg you have worked hard to save. Again, I caution you that

LOANS

these payments continue and you must plan for their payoff in your budget.
◆ Credit rating is an important tool in this new world we live in. Taking out a small loan may be the only way for a newly single person to start their credit rating status. Or, sometimes, it is the only way to establish or improve a problem that already exists. Either way, do it cautiously. Check into the background of any company that advertise "We will help you establish your credit."
◆ Opportunity knocks at unexpected times. It could come in the form of a business venture, an investment opportunity, or an item on sale for which you have been saving. Check any opportunity. Do not let your emotions make the decision for you.
◆ Convenience in traveling, for business expenses, etc. It's to easy to hand the credit card for payment. Use caution when using any credit card because you will have to pay the bill even if it was last month you ate the food.

WRONG REASONS FOR BORROWING:
◆ Short life span products such as vacation, dinning out and entertainment. Nothing is more draining on your budget than making payments long after the joy of a vacation has worn off. Plan ahead and put money aside to pay the bill when it comes.
◆ Basic expenses are your cost of living, food, clothing, shelter, utilities, day to day expenses, etc. Using credit for these is a warning signal of credit abuse and tells you that you are living beyond your means. If you do use a credit card, make sure you pay it off each month when the bill arrives.

- ◆ Gambling money borrowed is unwise, unhealthy and foolhardy. If you must gamble whether it is on a card game, bingo, stock market or whatever, use only money you can afford to lose.
- ◆ Impulse purchases are purchases with your emotions doing the buying instead of your brain. Stores and sales people play to these emotions. You must comparison shop and avoid impulse buying that runs up your debt burden.

MORTGAGE AND HOME EQUITY LOANS:
- ◆ Sale Contract: Make sure there is a time limit for a loan commitment (usually 30 days). If you need more time before the closing, ask and be sure to change the contract to reflect this. (i.e. 45-60 days)
- ◆ Avoid pressure to finalize your mortgage loan until you are ready.
- ◆ Any acceleration clause is like a demand note to force you to pay off the remaining balance early. This can be triggered by several different events such as, nonpayment of taxes or required home insurance, lack of permission to allow rental of home, late or nonpayment of a mortgage as due, sale of what is commonly known as a wrap around mortgage, etc.
- ◆ Federal laws do not allow the terms of a mortgage agreement to be changed. Read your current one carefully to see if there are any clauses that might restrict you. If you are signing a new mortgage, carefully read all clauses before you sign.
- ◆ Mortgages:
    1. **Fixed rate mortgage:** A level rate of interest throughout the term of the loan. As inter-

ests fluctuate in the market, this rate will remain constant. The only way to lower the interest it is to refinance with a new mortgage. Refinancing requires you to pay the costs for new appraisals, points, documentary stamps, etc. Unless you plan on living in the house for at least three to five years, it probably will not pay you to refinance.

2. Adjustable rate mortgages (known as ARMs): These mortgages have a changing rate of interest depending on the "prime rate of interest." Your payment will go up or down depending on whether the prime interest goes up or down. Lenders count on you to not know when you are overcharged on an adjustable mortgage. If you feel this has happened, write to the lender by certified mail, return receipt and make your complaint and tell where the problem is. There are mortgage auditing firms that, for a fee, will check your ARM to make sure you are not being overcharged.

3. Reverse Mortgages: American homeowners over the age of 62 can use the equity in their homes with a reverse mortgage. The loan uses the equity in your home as security. You must actually be living in the home. Recent legislation has opened the market for the reverse mortgage business. Here are some general items to consider before signing this type of loan.

What will best meet your needs?
- A one-time lump sum payment.

- Monthly payments to you over a period of time.
- A line of credit to be used if and when needed.

Do you need?
- A supplement to your income.
  - Money to make home improvements or major repairs.
  - Eliminate a house payment.
  - Money to hire help for medical or custodial care.

Consider also:
- How much equity will you have left after the payments to you are finished?
- Do you need to receive payments figured on your life expectancy?
- Payments to you are tax-free and do not affect your Social Security.

A benefit of a reverse mortgage loan means you retain the ownership of the home in your name. You will be making no monthly payment and there is no qualifying of income.

4. Second mortgages: A second mortgage is just as the name implies. It is a mortgage that has no rights until the first mortgage is paid in full. Because of this, lenders are reluctant to lend money when there is very little equity over and above what is on the first mortgage. The rate for these loans is much higher than a first mortgage.

5. **Home equity loans** (sometimes called a home equity line of credit): With a home equity loan you can borrow a set dollar

amount at a fixed interest rate. You can take a partial amount or have a lump sum payment. Either way you pay interest on the amount used. Repayment terms will be set and you will know exactly what your monthly payment will be. The interest you pay on this loan is deducted on your income tax the same as your regular home mortgage. Remember, if you can't make the payments you are in risk of losing your home. A home equity loan can:
- Provide a solid foundation for the extra funds you require.
- Can be used for a variety of purposes such as education, remodeling, debt consolidation, etc.

6. Balloon mortgage: These loans are fixed for a certain period of time (usually 3,5,10 years) and then become payable in full. This means you must come up with the balance owed or make another financing arrangement.
7. **FHA loans** (Federal Housing Authority): A FHA loan is a government loan given to low or moderate income families to assist them in purchasing homes. The interest rates are usually lower. They are easier to qualify for and require less of a down payment. Not all mortgage bankers or brokers are capable of obtaining these specialized loans.

PERSONAL LOANS:
◆ Line of credit: Usually used by a business to have money available as needed. In order to have this

open ended loan, pre-qualification is necessary. Both the lender and the borrower should make sure that all terms of the agreement are listed on the loan.
- ◆ Demand note agreement: Some companies require this clause in their personal loans instead of a specific time frame. It allows the lender to call the loan at any time.
- ◆ Signature loan: This is a loan without any collateral. You must qualify your credit rating before any institution will give you a loan. Interest is higher for any loan without backup security.
- ◆ Promissory note: A note that will address "who owes," "how much," "to whom," and "how" the money is to be repaid. A promissory note is a simple document that lists basic terms of the transaction:
    1. Amount of money lent to the borrower.
    2. Interest charged.
    3. Date and names of parties.
    4. Time and amount of payments.
- ◆ Automobile financing: Look for competitive rates and terms in financing any automobile. Some suggestions are your credit union, through the dealer, bank, etc. Be sure to read the sales agreement and the contract carefully. Watch for when the interest begins, whether it is on the date of delivery or on the date of purchase. Also be sure to check on any possible rebate, discount terms, option clauses or any other benefit the dealer allows and whether the terms are still in effect at the date of delivery.
- ◆ Automobile lease agreements: Cost is the difference between the original price and the residual

value plus lease charges. The longer the lease, the lower the payments. A down payment also reduces the monthly cost. This still is money paid out without any benefit at the end of the term. Lease agreements specify the amount of miles allowed each year. (Usually between 12,000 and 15,000 miles.) Any miles over the limit carries an extra charge plus charges for excessive wear and tear.

Check the terms of the lease contract carefully. What happens if the lease holder dies? What is the purchase price if you decide to buy the car? How is the liability insurance covered and by whom? Are there restrictions on who may drive?

CREDIT CARDS:

Credit cards are fast and convenient, but like all credit or loans, there can also be problems and precautions to take. (See Chapter 10 "Credit Cards")

> **HINT:** *Your credit rating will be checked whenever you make a loan application.*

RETIREMENT PLANS:

Some 401(k) and 403(b) plans have borrowing privileges. Sometimes they will lend up to 50% of the amount accumulated. They are easily accessible and there is no loan application or approval needed. One of the advantages of borrowing from your retirement plan, instead of a withdrawal, is that it is not taxable.

On the other hand, if you leave your employment for any reason before paying the amount back it becomes fully taxable. You will also be penalized 10% if you are under 59 ½ years old. You will be losing any interest or appreciation of that amount while it is withdrawn. Weigh your options carefully before you touch your retirement plan.

INSURANCE POLICIES:

Whole life insurance policies allow owners to borrow on the cash value of their insurance policies. Although it is at a low interest rate, it is an easy loan to forget about and to let the interest due accumulate. It will also be deducted from any pay off benefit of the policy. Know what you want before borrowing on your policy. (See Chapter 5, "Insurance")

The new law allows a withdrawal of the death benefit earlier if you have a terminal or serious illness. Contact your insurance agent for more information on this benefit.

MEMBERSHIPS:

Some of these you might not consider to be loan equivalencies. I have put them here because of the amount usually required to join. If you are borrowing money to join, make sure you know what you are joining and that you are able to pay back the money.

- ◆ Health clubs: Make sure the club is there to stay. Check their credentials, time in business, and get references. Some memberships are by the month or year. Be very careful if there is a large fee and a signed contract or if they start using high sale pressure methods. Read any contract to see what will happen if you are unable to continue for a health problem, move, or facility change. Is there a right to cancel at any time or will you be penalized?
- ◆ Fraternal organizations: These are long term com-

LOANS

mitments usually with a small up front amount plus monthly or annual dues. Most are beneficial.
◆ Social clubs: Large initial payment are required and usually are not transferable. Some have yearly dues and a minimum amount required to be spent per month in the club.

LENDERS:

Shop for the best place to borrow. This can vary depending on the need and the availability. Each type of loan has different rates and each financial institution has their own set up. You will pay more for a signature loan than for a car loan. The rate for an unsecured loan is always more than one that allows them to take property for nonpayment. (No asset to back up the loan.)
◆ Banks
◆ Saving and loan associations
◆ Consumer finance companies
◆ Credit unions
◆ Sales financial companies (they buy finance installment loans from retailers.)
◆ Government agencies
◆ Retirement funds
◆ Life insurance policies
◆ Pawnbrokers (last resort)

> **HINT:** *Late payments can be viewed as a warning signal to your lender that your loan will default. If payments are more than 30 days late they will probably be reported to a credit agency.*

SUGGESTED ORDER IN WHICH TO PAY BILLS:
- ◆ Pay the food and essential medical expenses. You must keep your family fed and healthy.
- ◆ Rent or housing expenses. This includes the utility bills.
- ◆ Car loans and expenses. You will need a car for transportation to work. Include in this all gas, oil, insurance and maintenance.
- ◆ Pay child-support current payment and add an amount to cover any past support. If you cannot pay the entire past due amount, contact the other party or attorney and make arrangements to catch up on the amount owed.
- ◆ Keep current with all income taxes. If you owe from a prior year, contact the IRS or state government to make arrangements to pay the amount. The government has the right to put a lien on your home or to garnish your wages.
- ◆ Pay payments on all secured loans. This means money you borrowed and put up collateral.
- ◆ Pay credit cards. If you are unable to pay a payment in full, call the company and make an arrangement with them for payment.

IDEAS TO CUT DEBTS:
- ◆ Put the credit cards away — prioritize what is important and pay cash or don't buy it.
- ◆ Use a budget — work out a budget and stick to it.
- ◆ Start savings — build up a fund for emergencies and large purchases.
- ◆ Shop around for a lower credit card rate.

Loans

- Cash advances on your credit card adds debt — avoid these and never get a cash advance from one card to pay another card.
- If necessary get a debt consolidation loan. This might save your credit, but it also may cost you more in the long run.
- Call the National Foundation for Consumer Credit, 800-388-2227, to find the nearest service. (They offer free or low cost counseling and education service on debt-reduction.)

CHAPTER

10

CREDIT CARDS AND CREDIT RATING

CREDIT CARDS AND CREDIT RATING

Credit cards are fast and convenient. There is no loan application and very litte waiting time. These little plastic cards can get you into real trouble. Use them with care and watch the interest charged on each card you have. Sometimes they say there is no interest for several months. Instead, you will find an up front fee. **Remember: they will make money somewhere.** Shop around for the lowest rate card. Often credit unions offer a card that has a carrying rate about 3 to 4 percent below other cards. Watch out for the offers you receive in the mail with a low interest rate. Consumer advocates advise that once the low rate expires the interest can double and even triple. Read the information carefully before accepting.

The mail is full of offers to get more cards. They say, "You are pre-approved for a Gold Card. Just sign the form enclosed and mail it back before the date listed below." They offer low interest rates but, as you start reading the fine print, it tells you the rate is only good for four months. Then what happens? Before returning the application, check the interest rates for months after the initial period and the yearly membership fee. You also will want to know the terms or penalties charged if you are a day or so late with your payment.

CREDIT CARDS AND CREDIT RATING

Here are some things to beware of:
- ◆ There are more fraudulent charges made during the Christmas holidays.
- ◆ Check your statements thoroughly and question any purchases with which you do not agree.
- ◆ Tear up all carbons.
- ◆ Always be sure you get your card back.

> **HINT:** *Whenever you use your credit card or identification, keep your wallet in your hand until you put the card back in your wallet.*

- ◆ Carry only the cards you intend to use and leave the rest safely at home.
- ◆ Never keep a card loose in your pocket. It is too easy to lose or have stolen.
- ◆ Check sales receipt and the total amount before signing.
- ◆ Keep all credit card receipts. Keep a separate file.
- ◆ MasterCard and Visa credit cards are marketed over the phone. They do not ask for confidential information at that time. If you are interested, they will mail you an application.
- ◆ Protect all your cards. It is a good idea to go to your local copy machine, take out everything in your wallet and copy both sides. Keep a copy with you when you travel and an extra copy in your file at home. That way if anything happens, you will have all the numbers and information immediately available. Other ways to protect your numbers are:
- ◆ Keep a list of all 800 numbers for credit cards and account numbers at home. You might add these

telephone numbers to the copies you have made.
- ◆ Don't ever give your credit card number to anyone over the phone unless you have called them or you know exactly who you are speaking to.
- ◆ Never write your credit card number on a check at purchase.

> **HINT:** *All reputable lenders require a credit check.*

CREDIT CARD DISPUTES:
1. Check to see if there are the words "National" or "N.A." next to the banks name. If there is, call 202-874-4820, the Consumer Complaint Hotline for the Comptroller of the Currency in Washington, D.C.
2. If you see the word "Savings" of "F. S. B." call 800-842-6929, the Office of Thrift Supervision.
3. If the words "Federal Credit Union" are next to the name then call 202-357-1000 to the National Credit Union Association.
4. Call 800-934-3342 to the Office of Consumer Affairs, F.D.I.C. if the word "State" is on the card.
5. If there is a problem with any other type of card, get in touch with you local attorney general's consumer protection office.

CREDIT RATING:
There are three major credit bureaus in this country. When applying for a loan or credit card, one or all of these will be contacted. If there is negative information in them, your application can be denied. Check with any or all of them to know if there are any problems.

Credit Cards and Credit Rating

Your bill paying history is being watched and recorded every day. Sometimes it is recorded wrong. With all the information available, mistakes are made. In fact, they are made quite often. You can correct them. It only takes one black mark to give you a credit problem. Contact them to get information you will need and the procedure you must follow to correct your account.

- ◆ Equifax: Office of Consumer Affairs, P.O. Box 105873, Atlanta, GA 30348; 800-685-1111.
- ◆ Trans Union: Consumer Relations Center, 760 W. Sproul Road, P.O. Box 350, Springfield, PA 19064; 610-690-4909.
- ◆ TRW Credit Data Division: National Consumer Relations Center, P.O. Box 8030, Layton, UT 84041; 800-682-7654.

The credit bureaus list late car payments, credit card installments, etc. They also record the total amount owed as well as the total limit amounts you can borrow on the accounts. From all the history of your account, they use a point system to see if you can qualify for the new application. Bills that are over 60 days late in payment can linger on your credit rating for 4-7 years. A few late payments won't do a lot of damage, but they will alert a lender to ask why.

You can pay all your bills in cash. You can even pay cash to buy the house you live in. The car in the garage can be paid in cash and the children can be sent to college by paying the tuition in cash. You can do this, but I don't believe anyone does or wants to. You must sometime have a need for a credit card or the ability to borrow money.

> **HINT:** *It is vital to have a credit card. You can't even rent a car without a credit card!*

If you have a bad credit rating or have never had a credit card before, there are reliable companies to help you. Talk to your bank or financial institution before using a TV advertised company. Be very skeptical about credit repair companies. They might claim they can wipe out negative information in your credit history. This is false and might even lead to giving fraudulent information. It takes time and successful negotiations with a creditor to erase the information.

> **CREDIT CARD TRAP:** *John is trying to stay afloat with a life style above his means. He runs up a hefty balance on his MasterCard. He then takes out a new Visa card and gets a cash withdrawal to pay the payment. Of course, it is easy to charge on the new Visa card as well as adding to the MasterCard. The next month rolls around and he takes out a Discover card so he can get a cash withdrawal to pay the payments on the other two cards. John is now getting in debt and is caught in the credit card trap.* **Beware!**

STEPS YOU CAN TAKE:
- ◆ Pay your bills on time. Lenders love an account that is flawless.
- ◆ Apply only when needed. When you apply to of-

ten for credit cards, you might be considered a "poor credit customer." It also is not a good idea to keep open large lines of credit.
- Use the same name. Don't use John Q. Public and then use J.Q. Public. Using several variations of your name allows more avenues for mistakes.
- If a problem in paying comes up, write or contact the company and make arrangements for payment. Discuss your problem with them and don't assume they know what is going on.
- Don't cosign. Keep your credit history separate from your spouse or any other person. That way if either of you has a problem, it will allow the other's credit as a backup.
- Check for mistakes when:
  1. Any dispute over a billing from a store, etc. that you have refused to pay, you should have your explanation on your report.
  2. Make sure that any judgment you have paid completely is removed, not only from the credit history, but from your local court recording department.
  3. When canceling credit cards, make sure the account indicates that the account was closed at your request.
  4. If you are separating or divorcing your spouse, make sure the companies close all joint accounts so that future charges by your spouse will not be in your name.
  5. List any slow pays and have an explanation before applying for a loan. Get a credit report on both the husband's and the wife's name if both will be signing for the loan.

> **HINT:** *Remember: Your credit history may affect your job, your ability to make an emergency loan, or even to purchase a simple item.*

For your information, I am quoting a column that appeared syndicated across the country on November 6, 1996, with special permission of the financial columnist Humberto Cruz. I start where he quotes from a letter he received from Stuart Blum, a certified public accountant,

> *"I think I can top your credit-card earnings. I use GM Card, earn 5 percent toward a new GM vehicle on my purchases, then pay the balance with a balance-transfer check from Chase, whose balance I then pay with a balance-transfer check from Wachovia, whose balance I then pay with a balance-transfer check from Citibank, etc.*
>
> *"These banks all treat a balance transfer like a purchase — that is, they charge no transaction fee or interest if the transfer is paid by the grace period."*
>
> **"Congratulations. I admire anyone who can milk money — legally, of course — from credit-card issuers who all too often are simply enticing people to stay in debt,"** Mr. Cruz **commented.** *(Emphasis added)*
>
> *"Obviously, whoever plays this game risks running out of balance-transfer checks at some point and having to come up with his or her own money. But, following your tactic, "is doable in*

CREDIT CARDS AND CREDIT RATING

today's market-place," said Robert B. McKinley, president of RAM Research Group in Frederick, Md., a company that tracks credit cards for industry executives and consumers.

"You can have your cake and eat it, too," McKinley said. "You just have to be organized, keep track of how much you owe to whom and make sure all payments are made on time."

(© *Tribune Media Services. All Rights Reserved. Printed with permission.*)

This is a far reaching example, but as you can see, it can be done. I don't advise it because as Mr. Cruz stated in another column, **"That's the cavalier attitude about credit-card debt that has put so many Americans in a financial hole. It's almost as if interest payments on credit cards have become an accepted and expected part of a family's budget."** (Emphasis added)

> *Note: Tucked into the tax legislation in 1997 is a provision that would allow the Federal government to accept credit, debit of charge cards for the payment of Federal income taxes. This provision creates another way to increase the balance and the interest you pay on your credit cards — BEWARE.*

Suddenly Alone

CHAPTER 11

LEGAL SERVICES

LEGAL SERVICES

An attorney may be the first person you have ever hired. It is vital to know what you want and what you expect in an attorney before making a final commitment. An attorney is a specialist and is not chosen like produce in a grocery store. It's like choosing a dress or tie for that special date coming up. It's chosen with care, so the fit will be just right.

NEVER SHARE AN ATTORNEY. It is a conflict of interest for an attorney to represent both of you. He can only be a knight in shining white armor for one. Both parties have a right and a need for individual, competent counsel.

An attorney will not be adverse to the discussion of legal fees and costs. In fact, any responsible attorney is happy to discuss his fees and costs with a client.

> **HINT:** *You are a consumer. Remember, the lawyer has a service to sell.*

Copy the form "ATTORNEYS" at the end of this chapter. In the first column, make a list of attorneys. Put their telephone numbers into the second column. Get recommendations from friends who have used an attorney for wills, estates, divorce etc. depending on your need. Other places you might look or call is the local bar association, minister, mediator, family counselor, special interest groups or the yellow pages.

Now you have a list of possible attorneys. It is time to do a little research, so you can get the best attorney for your particular need. Take out a sheet of paper. Start listing questions you want answered in your first telephone call, questions about costs, retainers, qualifications, availability, etc. Organize this list of questions, so they fall into a natural sequence. Here is a possible list:
1. Do you work in the field of __?__ law? (? = your need i.e. probate, will, trust)
2. What percentage of your practice is __?__ ?
3. What is the charge for an initial consultation?
4. Do you require a retainer agreement?
5. How much retainer money is needed up front?
6. Do you charge by the hour, and if so, how much?
7. Are your fees negotiable?
8. Are you available in case of emergency?
9. What about confidentiality?
10. May I make an appointment?

Call each number on your list. Identify yourself, tell the secretary that you are thinking about __?__ and have questions about hiring an attorney. Ask to talk to the attorney. This is how you can find if the attorney will be available to you later and how cooperative he will be. Note any answers and be sure to answer any questions he puts to you.

As you make these calls, you will eliminate those attorneys who do not work in __?__ law or that you do not feel comfortable with. Don't feel badly about this. You are a possible client, and their legal advice and services are for sale. You don't have to buy. Make appointments with the ones you think you can work with and believe can do the job. If the attorney is unavailable for an initial interview, he is not for you. You want an attorney who is interested enough to talk to you.

In the third column note the day and time of the appointment. When you have finished with all the telephone calls, you will have set up a few appointments.

Take time now and sort through everything you have learned. You have discovered a lot about each and what representation is available. If there are some attorneys that are questionable, cancel these appointments.

> **HINT:** *You can say "NO" and look elsewhere. There are a lot of attorneys available.*

Check with your particular state bar association to ask if there have been any complaints against the remaining lawyers. The local yellow pages will list a telephone number. You will also want to make sure each attorney is in good standing and licensed by the state.

The important time has arrived. Narrow your search down to a maximum of three attorneys. You are now ready to interview them. Put together a short synopsis of your case, making sure you include important dates, minor children, income, present living arrangements and present working status. Show him you are prepared as you expect him to be.

This is the time for you to find out more about the attorney. It is the time for you to decide if you want to hire him and for him to decide if he wants to take you on as a client.

LEGAL SERVICES

> **HINT:** *An attorney does not have to take your case.*

Again, it is good to have a list of questions or ideas. There are many areas that can cause future confusion. It is important not to be so intent on asking questions that you don't listen to the answers. Repeat any question that was not fully answered in your initial phone call or that you didn't understand. Depending on your needs, questions might include:

1. Ask for definite information on fees, whether by the hour, a flat rate fee by the case, a combination of both, any extras, and the expected total.
2. Check what costs are involved, such as filing, process serving, witnesses, experts, appraisals, depositions, copies, etc.
3. What are the charges for office visits, hearings, depositions, phone calls, letters, etc?
4. How is the fee arrangement handled? Is there a retainer up front? How will I be billed and the balance paid? It is wise to get this in writing.
5. Must I sign a retainer agreement?
6. Are the filing and court costs to be paid up front?
7. Are you available in a crisis?

> **HINT:** *Obviously, your goal should be to get legal representation and to avoid drawn-out, legal entanglements.*

8. Am I charged when I talk to the secretary? If so, under what conditions and how much?

9. How long do you think this will take?
10. Will you be handling this yourself, or will you turn it over to an associate?
11. Do you promptly answer or return phone calls?
12. Can I just give a message to your secretary?
13. What are my legal options?

Not all of these questions will apply to you. Use as many ideas as you need. After the interview, use column four to decide which attorney you want. Try not to let it be an emotional decision. Make notes in this column until you make up your mind. Possibly a lawyer new to the profession will be able to handle this less expensively. Think back on all the answers and then take the big step. Hire the one that will work best for you. Do this at the earliest possible time.

HINT: *Be prepared and be informed.*

The attorney is not there to hold your hand and listen to all the small complaints. He is there to protect your interests and to do the best possible job. Don't take up his time with small talk and emotional issues. It will only cost you more money.

The law, while it has rules, allows the judges a lot of discretion. Any good lawyer knows that nothing is definite if the court is allowed to make the decisions for you. Work hard to settle everything before a court hearing. If not, settle as many issues as possible before going to court.

If you find during the process that you are not being represented as you expect, you have the right to dismiss your attorney. You can find a replacement with

LEGAL SERVICES

whom you can work well. Don't tolerate halfway measures. Demand the best. Do not allow an attorney to dominate, scream or verbally abuse you. The attorney has a duty to represent you to the best of his ability. Take an active role in protecting your interests.

> **HINT:** *You have a right to hire and fire an attorney if you feel it is necessary to protect your rights.*

RETAINERS AND RETAINER AGREEMENTS

Normally, a retainer fee will be required up-front. Each attorney requires a different amount before representing you. Before you pay this, ask about the total charges and what will be expected of you. Will the attorney work on a "flat fee" arrangement or will he be charging by the hour? If he charges by the hour, check to make sure he will itemizes each billing.

The fee the attorney charges sets the standard of value for time and services in representing you. It is much easier for the attorney to collect at the beginning than at the end. He knows this and will make every effort to get as much as he can in advance.

Costs of any legal action will not be paid by the attorney. These costs include filing fees, discovery, service of papers, appraisals, etc. Make sure that you know how these costs will be paid and if they will be billed separately.

> **HINT:** *Separate checks should be made out to cover costs and legal fees.*

If there is an unused portion of the retainer fee left at the end of representation, who gets it? Check to see if you will receive a refund if for some reason you change attorneys. Some attorneys will make arrangements to return any overage while others maintain that it was paid for their availability and representation.

It is practical for an attorney to require you to sign a retainer agreement. It may not be practical for you to sign it. Any retainer agreement should specify exactly the way fees will be charged, when and how much. If you decide not to sign the agreement, follow up with a letter to the attorney stating the fees and charges as you understand them. The letter should spell out the understanding of how the fees will be paid and how they are to be billed. Make note of any special representation agreed on or experts to be hired. This letter will protect both you and the attorney and will prevent any misunderstandings later. It will confirm your agreement without giving away any of your other rights.

Any retainer agreement should be signed prior to representation. You will have no negotiating power on fees or services later. Any agreement signed after representation has started can be taken as overreaching and coercive.

> **HINT:** *Don't allow yourself to be pushed into signing a retainer agreement that is unfair to you.*

Beware of the fine print in a retainer agreement. Each attorney writes his own, so naturally it is written to protect him. You **MUST** read it carefully. Never sign it on a first visit. Take it home and go over it cautiously.

LEGAL SERVICES

> **HINT:** *Read the retainer agreement before signing. (See sample agreement at end of this chapter.)*

Sometimes you will find that there are built in security devices for the attorney. This can be in the form of an automatic lien against your home for non-payment. Maybe it requires you to sign a note secured by your home or another piece of real estate.

Another device the attorney uses is to write into the agreement that his fee will come directly off the top of any amount you receive by whatever means. This in itself sounds fair, but be wary! That way he receives his fee no matter how much he charges, and you may end up with nothing.

> **HINT:** *Watch out for pitfalls that protect only the attorney.*

A retainer agreement can contain these points:
1. Receipt of any money paid and where it is applied, such as costs and fees.
2. How fees are charged, computed and billed.
3. Any charges that are costs. (i.e. filing, research, specific services, mailing, copies, experts, etc.)
4. Detail the attorney's duties and how they will be handled, that is, the list of services expected to be performed.
5. An understanding that no settlement will be made without your written consent.
6. Duration of the agreement. State when representation ends.

7. The fee difference between court and office time.
8. Any interest charged on the unpaid balance.
9. If there is a dispute between you and the attorney, how will it be resolved.
10. Costs entailed if the attorney has to force collection and who will be required to pay these costs.
11. Provisions for a change in attorneys, for whatever reason, and the fee for forwarding your records to your new attorney.

> **HINT:** *Attorneys sometimes will not release vital records without full payment of any existing bill.*

12. When there is a change in attorneys, will a lien be put on the documents, property, or money in the attorney's possession until the bill is paid.
13. An understanding of whether the attorney will be handling the whole case himself or will any other person be involved, that is, another attorney or legal assistant/paralegal.
14. The tax deductibility of any portion of the fee.
15. If someone else is ordered to pay legal fees and costs, how this will be handled?
16. Signature of attorney and client and date of agreement.

READ THE AGREEMENT WITH GREAT CARE!

NOTE: *If you are not being represented as you think you should be, change attorneys.*

NOTE: *Only you can make sure your rights are protected.*

LEGAL SERVICES

PREPAID LEGAL SERVICES

Memberships are available for pre-paid legal services through several large companies. These providers usually give you unlimited phone consultations. Many times all you need is to ask a question. This not only saves time and expense for the attorney, but it is cost effective for you. Legal services they provide can include:

- Unlimited phone consultations 24 hours a day.
- One letter written on a particular matter. (Usually this can take care of a problem.)
- Wills. (Family members at a low cost.)
- Representation in your local community at low rates.
- Specified hours of representation for some services. (i.e. civil or criminal action, personal injury cases, driver's license protection, etc.)

ELDER LAW

Elder law concentrates on legal issues relating to people over the age of 55. These lawyers seek to provide each client with information and services in the ever growing complex issues of "growing older."

In *Webster's New World Dictionary* the word elder means older, of superior rank and position, an older person with some authority. With that in mind, the field of elder law opens up questions of the documents and choices the elder population must face. Some of these problems deal with long term care, passing of assets from one generation to another, planning to avoid tax consequences, trusts, etc. You may be wise to take advantage of their expertise for your estate planning.

Attorneys
(Make a copy of this form.)

Name	Telephone	Time and Date	Decision

LEGAL SERVICES

SAMPLE RETAINER AGREEMENT

JONES, JONES, SMITH, & WESSON, P.A.

CLIENT:
MATTER:
DATE:

I hereby agree to employ the above law firm to represent me in connection with_____. I authorize you to do and perform all acts on my part which are necessary and appropriate in this representation. I understand that this agreement covers legal representation for the above mentioned matter only. It does not include appeals, petition for modification of any final judgment, or any contempt proceedings or other post-trial proceedings. Then additional arrangements will have to be made. In the absence of a separate agreement, any such post-judgment work performed by this law firm will be billed at the rates specified in this agreement.

I agree to pay you as compensation for your professional services a minimum sum of $_____. That entire sum shall be paid as a retainer, of which $_____ is non-refundable. The non-refundable portion of this fee includes the initial conference, the evaluation of your case, and its undertaking and is consideration for the attorney's agreement to accept employment, to assure the availability of that attorney and/or his associates, and that accepting such retainer precludes that attorney's employment by or for any adverse party. It is understood that the retainer shall be deposited for the payment of fees. The minimum charge is only a minimum fee, and additional fee may be charged based upon such factors as the time and labor required, the results accomplished, the amount *in controversy, the novelty and difficulty of the matter, the skill required to perform the legal service properly, and the experience, reputation and ability of the lawyer or lawyers performing this service for me. I realize I am being charged for time spent on my case including time spent for conferences, telephone calls, drafting of documents, negotiations, legal research, court time and travel to and from locations from the lawyer's office. I understand that it is the practice of your office to compute not less than 1/5 of an hour for each telephone call, no matter its duration.*

I fully understand that, as to that portion of the attorney's fees based upon an hourly rate, the hourly rate which I am obligating myself for is : $_____ per hour for David Jones, $____per hour for John Smith and Jane Smith and $__ per hour for the services of law clerks and/or paralegal personnel.

I understand that it is impossible at this time to determine the total amount of my attorney's fee.

You are authorized to incur liability for all expenses, such as long distance telephone calls, photocopies, and out of town travel expenses, court reporter expenses, including cost of transcript and court reporter's fee for attendance, court costs, such as filing fees, service of process, newspaper publication, subpoena costs, witness fees, recording fees, etc., accounting and appraisal fees, and expenses for other experts which you deem necessary to assist in preparation for and trial of my case. I have advanced you a cost deposit of $_____ towards these expenses which is separate from the attorney fee retainer. I understand you will endeavor, prior to incurring any major costs, to explain these costs to me.

I understand that I will be billed periodically for the time spent on my case, both as to attorney and paralegal fees, after my initial retainer fee has been used, and that I will also be billed for expenses incurred. I fully agree to pay my bill

LEGAL SERVICES

promptly upon receipt. If I have any disagreement about the amount of the bill, I will advise you in writing in ten days; otherwise, I agree to the amount of your bill to the date of the billing statement. I understand that any bill that is not paid in full within thirty days of being billed will draw interest at the rate of 1 1/2% per month. I further agree that my entire fees and expenses are my personal responsibility and that I must keep them current and pay them in full to you before my case goes to final hearing.

I understand that you, as my attorney have the right to withdraw from this case if I do not make the payments required by this agreement or in the event I have misrepresented or failed to disclose any material fact, and you shall be compensated for that work which has been performed. In the event that this contract is terminated, a bill for services to date will be rendered which shall be payable upon receipt.

Sometimes the court orders one party to pay all or some of the fees and costs of the other. If the party pays all or some of the fees, it will be credited to my account, but will not limit the fee nor my obligation to pay this fee. Any effort to enforce collection is billable to me notwithstanding the fact that the court may order the fee paid directly to Jones, Jones, Smith & Wesson, P.A.

The provisions of this agreement, in the attorney's discretion, may be disclosed to the court in connection with any application for fees for services that may be rendered on my behalf, and you have the right to advise the court of any amounts that you have received on account of fees and any security given you to secure your fees.

You shall have a lien on all of my documents, property, or money in your possession for the payment of all sums due to you from me under the terms of this agreement. In addition, I hereby consent to a charging lien insuring that, if you elect, payment will come from the recovery, that is, out of the results or fruits of litigation in the event it is not otherwise paid. In the event it is necessary to institute collection activities against me, I agree to pay all attorney's fees and costs incurred by you which are necessitated by my non-payment.

I acknowledge that you have made no guarantee concerning the outcome of this case and that all expressions relative to the results hoped for are merely made in your professional opinion, given the facts and law known to you at the time the opinions are rendered.

I have reviewed and fully understand this agreement. All of my questions concerning this agreement have been asked and answered.

Date at_____, this_____ day of_____, 199___.

_____   _____

Client   *Jones, Jones, Smith & Wesson*

LEGAL SERVICES

Letter Confirming Representation

Street Address _____
City _____ State _____ Zip _____

Date _____

_____ , Esquire
Street Address _____
City _____ State _____ Zip _____

    Re: Name v. Name

Dear (Name):

    This letter serves as confirmation of our oral agreement reached on _____, 199 __, wherein I agreed to retain your law firm for (list type of action here i.e. wills, divorce, etc.)

    I have agreed to pay for you to commence your representation for $_____.__ as a (refundable/non-refundable) minimum fee. I agree to pay you $__.__ per hour, after this minimum is used, to be billed and itemized monthly. Any fees for paralegals or experts will be agreed to in advance. I understand that the monthly bills are to be paid timely.

    This acknowledges your receipt of $_____.__ paid on this date.

    I agreed to pay, in addition to the hourly fees for professional services, the out of pocket expenses that are necessary. These will include photocopies, court reporter fees, long distance calls, courier services, filing fees, service of subpoenas, etc.

I understand that there are no guarantees as to the outcome of this matter and that you were not able to advise me as to the total costs.

We have agreed that I will be notified for approval of any settlement and hearings. I will also be notified before any extension of time or change of hearing is made and any change will require my approval.

Please acknowledge our agreement by signing the enclosed copy of this letter and returning it to me in the self addressed envelope. I look forward to a conclusion of this matter.

Sincerely,

Your name
Your telephone number

ACCEPTED AND AGREED:

Dated

CHAPTER 12

※

CONTRACTS

CONTRACTS

Everything we do requires a contract of some kind. It started when we were children. The contracts were oral, but they were contracts. Your mother said, "You do the dishes tonight and I will do them tomorrow." Your part of the contract was doing the dishes tonight. You fulfilled your part of the oral contract. Your mother fulfilled her part on the next night when she washed the dishes. This is what is known as a simple contract.

Even the school had a contract with you. "You do all the homework, attend the classes, do well on the tests and we will give you a grade according to the effort you set forth." Simple contracts like this are a daily occurrence.

Purchasing a new television is another type of contract. The dealer says, "I will sell you this set for $350 and I will warrant it for a full year." You accept the offer and pay him the money, fulfilling your part of the contract. He gives you the television set. The rest of his part of the contract will take a year to complete. If the set has a problem and the dealer does not honor the warranty, per the contract, then there are legal steps that you can take.

Then marriage came along and you entered into another contract. There may be other words used than the love, honor and obey. It is still a contract under the laws of this country. Like many contracts, it takes legal action to cancel.

Contracts are also ones we sign. The purchase and payment agreement for a new automobile is a good example. It's usually a couple of pages long, typed and in very small print. I bet at this point, not more than 5% of the people read the complete contract. That's scary when you think maybe the small print could give away your first born. The contract is the agreement, not what the salesman told you, not the terms you think are there. The agreement is only what is written in the contract.

CONTRACT REQUIREMENTS:
- ◆ Offer: An offer is a communication either written or oral which creates in the offeree the power to form a contract by accepting in an authorized manner. It must be a manifestation of willingness to enter into a bargain, so made as to justify another person in understanding that his assent to that bargain is invited and will conclude the matter.
- ◆ Acceptance: The offeror is the master of the offer and may dictate the manner and means by which the offer is to be accepted. In order to accept, the terms and manner of acceptance must be followed. If they are not, then there will be a counter offer and there must be an acceptance by the other party to these different terms.
- ◆ Consideration: In simple terms, consideration is the price paid for the promise. Each party has a price. As an example — for one it may be money for goods and for another it might be a promise to do something for pay.

> **HINT:** *A contract must have an understanding or meeting of the minds of the terms and conditions.*

WRITTEN CONTRACTS:

The Federal and state governments have laws that require all contracts over a certain amount of money or over a certain length of time to be in writing. All real estate contracts must be in writing. Other contracts that need to be in writing are, for example, a promise to pay a debt for someone else or an agreement for leasing for a period longer than a year.

- ◆ Watch out for words like agree, stipulate, promote, covenant, automatically, etc. This makes a contract binding, despite what the salesman will tell you.
- ◆ Watch out for phrases such as homestead rights, assignment of wages or pensions, agent's fees, direct deposit, payment of legal fees, a waiver of any right, etc.
- ◆ Watch the details and fine print, consult an attorney if you have any doubt about what you are signing and **always keep a copy.**
- ◆ If you change anything in a contract, be sure to initial the change and have the other party initial it also.

> **HINT:** *Don't just sign any contract handed to you. (You can change the terms or wording before signing if you both agree.)*

ORAL CONTRACTS:
- This includes most store purchases, meetings with others and handshake contracts.
- Contracts must be completed in a certain length of time and under a certain amount of money. (See WRITTEN CONTRACTS on the previous page)
- Just because you are friends, does not mean a handshake is a valid contract. Be wary and put your terms and agreement in writing.

PROBLEMS:
Not all contracts work out the way we expect or want them to. Material and goods might not be delivered, money may not be paid and we might change our minds. Some of the more frequent problems are:
- No actual agreement or meeting of the minds.
- Financially irresponsible party. (On either side)
- Bankruptcy of one of the parties.
- Disappearance of one of the parties.
- Nonpayment.
- Unforeseen circumstances.
- Non-licensed contractor.

As you can see, it is important for both parties in a contract to know exactly the terms of the agreement. It can be expensive and time consuming to enforce a contract. Know what you are doing before entering into a written or oral contract. Remember: it is his word against yours if you must enforce the contract in court.

Non-Contract?

Jenny and Rich decided to publish a newsletter. Jenny did all the research and wrote the copy. She also set the type and arranged for the printing. Rich sold the subscriptions, did the mailing and contacted advertisers. For one of the issues Jenny bought two drawings from a local artist. When she picked them up she paid the price asked. While she noticed the little artist's copyright mark on the drawings, she knew she had paid for them in full.

The drawings were used for the newsletter. A year later she reused the drawings in another publication and the artist sued her for a second payment on what he called his "copyrighted drawings".

Moral to this story is that nothing was put into a formal contract. Jenny has her canceled check on the payment for the drawings. The artist only has his word that he kept the copyright. It is still in the courts and costing both parties lots of money. Only the legal system knows how this will turn out.

CHAPTER

13

✳

ESTATE PLANNING

ESTATE PLANNING

The old saying is true — nothing can stop taxes or dying and you can't take it with you. As long as you have something that is important to you, you must have a will to make sure it goes to the person intended. The need for a will becomes even more important in our American Society as we tend to live much longer and have more complicated financial situations and second families. Rising real estate values, stock values, retirement benefits and increasing family members make your decisions more complex. Now is the time to make your plans about how and what you want. Make it easier for your heirs and survivors. The price you pay now is low compared to the costs your survivors will pay later.

The emotional trauma at the death or divorce of a spouse or the loss of a family member is only a part of what one must go through. The accompanying financial and legal problems are sometimes more than a person can handle alone. Emotions can drive the money decisions and these may not be the right decisions. If at all possible, make plans well ahead of time to lessen the transition for one of you to be left alone. Work out arrangements, make your family aware of what you want and keep it simple enough for them to understand. There are many "tools" available to use in your estate

Estate Planning

planning. Such "tools" can be ownership of assets with rights of survivorship, designated beneficiaries, powers of attorney, revocable and irrevocable trusts, homestead rights and a will.

> HINT: *The foundation of your estate planning should be a will and/or revocable trust.*

Your "estate" is all the wealth you have accumulated during your lifetime. This is true no matter how little or how extensive your assets are. It includes all your real and personal property combined. Even a modest estate may be subject to probate. By making your own arrangements you can help your heirs avoid conflict, delays and unnecessary expenses.

Probate is your state's court proceedings required to conclude the legal and financial matters of a deceased person. Through this court process the probate creditors are paid and the remainder of your estate is distributed to your heirs. Probate can be very time consuming, expensive and can tie up the assets until the proceedings are completed.

Probate is also a matter of public record. Anyone can walk into the courthouse and discover exactly how much the deceased owned and who he owed. This opens an avenue for potential sales persons or unscrupulous persons to promote their products and services. It gives nosey neighbors a chance to check the records.

> HINT: *Unless you are very knowledgeable, do not make out your will by yourself or with a form you might be able to buy.*

Your goal in making out an estate plan is to allow your assets to pass to your survivors with a minimum of cost, time and confusion. The more of the following questions you can answer yes, the less your probate procedure will cost in time and money as well as giving your survivors a plan to follow.

- ◆ Have you made out an estate plan?
- ◆ Is your will current and the beneficiaries accurate?
- ◆ Is the will a self-proving will?
- ◆ Is there an alternate or second beneficiary listed in the will and other documents?
- ◆ Are all the surviving children also the children of the surviving spouse?
- ◆ Have you made any plans for children of a previous marriage or relationship?
- ◆ Is anything listed in the will or documents unusual in any way?
- ◆ Will the debts be paid without delay?
- ◆ Have you made any plans in the case of your incapacity?

> **HINT:** *Estate planning isn't just for people with money. It's for everyone who cares about their families.*

- ◆ Is there a trust in effect to transfer assets to beneficiaries?
- ◆ Do you have a living will and/or a durable power of attorney?
- ◆ Are all the beneficiaries current on your life insurance and/or retirement plans?
- ◆ Have you made arrangements for your home and personal property to be safeguarded?

◆ Do your survivors know where to find all the documents?

DOCUMENTS TO LOOK FOR IN A GOOD ESTATE PLAN:
◆ Current will.
◆ Trust documents.
◆ Living will.
◆ Durable power of attorney.
◆ Naming of a guardian if incapacitated.
◆ Preference of Personal Representative.
◆ Guardian for minor children.
◆ Funeral instructions.
◆ Burial instructions.

THE MAIN WAYS TO TRANSFER ASSETS AT THE TIME OF DEATH:
1. By will — Your formal declaration in writing which transfers title to your property at death. It tells your heirs what you want done with your affairs and transfers your assets to the person or persons you designate. Everything you pass by will goes through probate.
2. By trust — A formal document encompassing titles of all your assets and giving the distribution to those you specify. Everything passes by the trust agreement and avoids probate but does not avoid estate taxes.
3. By joint tenancy (joint ownership) — Title is held in two names with rights of survivorship. The last surviving tenant owns the property outright.
4. Intestate (without a will) — The state will decide who among the family members inherits the prop-

erty and in what proportions. When you die intestate, the state will distribute by statute all assets. Any property in trust or joint ownership transfers assets to the inheriting survivors without probate.
5. By designating a beneficiary — This is done by insurance companies, retirement funds and automatically avoids probate.

Estate planning is overlooked by more people and constantly put off because it's not time to do that yet. Who knows what is the time? It is a sure bet that there are choices; plan to leave your money to family and friends, give it to a charity of your choice, or let the tax man, the lawyer, and the banks get most of it.

Another reason people put off estate planning is they think they don't have enough money to worry about. Maybe they don't have enough for them to worry about but, if plans for the transfers of what little they have aren't made, there may not be anything left for anyone.

Examples:

John is married and has three children. He wants to take care of his wife, but he also wants his children to share the assets. He also doesn't want any fighting over the division of his assets. Rather than the estate being forced to sell any of the assets, he divides the assets by will, specifying which asset he wants to go to each person. Then each has control and can sell the asset or keep it as the person sees fit without affecting the other heirs.

Estate Planning

> John is married and has three children. He wants his wife to have all the assets and the income to live on. He put both their names on most of the assets and his will specifies her as beneficiary of everything else. Or he can put the assets in a trust and list her as the beneficiary.
>
> John is married and has two children by a former marriage. He wants his wife to have the income and the control of the assets when he is gone. He also wants to make sure that after her death his children will receive the remainder of the assets. He does this with a legally drawn up trust. This trust transfers the assets without the long drawn out probate process.

It's important to anticipate your spouse's death or disability as well as your death or disability. What problems will your family have to face? Is your will current and can it be contested? What plans have you made if you are incapacitated? These are only a few of the problems that can be averted with advanced preparations.

It is estimated that two out of every three persons will die without a will. Many of these have no possessions or have their assets titled with another person or entity. These joint ownerships transfer without probate. Retirement funds and life insurance with living beneficiaries also transfer without probate. The key words here are "living beneficiaries." If you fail to keep your funds or policy beneficiaries up to date, the proceed will go into your estate and be transferred by will or state statute by the probate court .

> **Hint:** *All financially savvy couples will list all the assets of their marriage, all separate assets of each, as well as all liabilities. Compiling will take time, but the effort is worthwhile. Once you have a basic list, it will be easy to upgrade periodically. (See Chapter 3 "Financial Statements")*

Follow the hint above and make out your list. Copy it and take it with you to consult an attorney who is knowledgeable in estates. (You might even want to consult an accountant or financial advisor) Also, take along your last three years tax forms. It would be a good idea to list some of the items you want to cover in your will or trust as well some of the problems you might anticipate. Be prepared with questions so you can better understand the process. Finally list the names, addresses, phone numbers, dates of birth, and relationship of all those you want to include.

The following is a list of documents to take to your meeting with an estate planner. Make a copy for him, then you will not pay for his time to make the copies. These are only suggestions and you may have less or more to consider.

- ◆ Your name(s), full address, telephone number, Social Security number, birth and marriage date.
- ◆ All current or prior wills and trusts.
- ◆ Current bank and investment statements.
- ◆ Financial statement (See Chapter 3 "Financial Statement").
- ◆ Copies of deeds to all real property including home.

- ◆ Employer benefit and pension information.
- ◆ Life insurance policy numbers, face value, company, premium amounts and application.
- ◆ Retirement plan statements. (401(k), IRA, SEP, Keough, etc.)
- ◆ Business ownership (share certificates, agreements, repurchase agreements or buy-sell agreements).
- ◆ Military retirement or discharge papers.
- ◆ Names, addresses, telephone numbers and Social Security numbers of all family members and friends who will be beneficiaries or heirs.
- ◆ List of possible plans of action.

DURABLE POWER OF ATTORNEY:

A very simple legal tool called a Durable Power of Attorney is available to ensure that your affairs and maintenance in case of disability or incompetence is taken care of. Use of this avoids the need for court appointed guardianships and conservatorship. You can allow a competent person of your choice to handle these important issues if and when they are needed. This power is used only during incapacity and expires if you regain capacity.

While there are many such forms available on the market, I suggest that you contact your attorney. The attorney knows some of the pitfalls and can eliminate them before they become a problem. You can revoke the durable power of attorney at anytime or execute an amendment to the document.

A Durable Power of Attorney allows you to be in charge of your own life and destiny. You are making the decisions, not the court, not someone not of your

choosing. This document can allow your attorney of fact to:
- ◆ Pay your bills, manage your finances, and open your mail.
- ◆ Manage, depose of, sell or convey real and personal property.
- ◆ Select medical care and options.
- ◆ Handle all checks or cash coming to you. Invest or sell as needed.
- ◆ File your taxes.
- ◆ Everything you could have done yourself.

As a safeguard, you can limit the issues the attorney of fact can do. You might want to limit any loans or mortgages on your property. Any limits you impose can protect you from becoming a victim of negligence, fraud or incompetence but, it can also hinder you from receiving proper care. This is your decision. Use a little foresight, ask questions and do what is right for you and your loved ones.

> **Hint:** *Be sure to have someone in charge of your home and belongings. Let them know where the key is and how many other keys there are. It is a good idea for them to change the locks immediately after death to secure your property.*

TRUSTS:
- ◆ Revocable living trust. Also, called a grantor, living trust or inter-vivos trust. A trust is essentially a contract where the grantor transfers his assets to a trustee who agrees to own, administer and distribute the assets to the designated beneficiaries

according to the provisions of the written trust agreement. Usually the grantor, the trustee and the beneficiary are the same person with the trust naming successor trustees and beneficiaries.
- ✓ While you are alive and competent, you have complete control over the assets of a living trust. You can sell, buy, hold, spend or whatever you want. While a will can contain provisions to transfer assets at death, a trust is effective during life and transfers assets at death immediately to the beneficiaries.
- ✓ A living trust allows the grantor flexibility and control over all the assets. Although you have relinquished the nominal ownership of these assets to the trust, you will continue to be the beneficial owner. You also have the right to change the terms of the trust or the beneficiaries. You can even revoke the trust anytime you choose.
- ✓ A trust is not part of the probate process. It does not go into the public record. A will must go through the probate court procedure and the assets, the heirs and what they have inherited becomes part of the public record. There are people out there that thrive on the court records. They make their money going after these heirs with schemes of all kinds. The assets though are included in the estate tax form with the IRS.
- ✓ An appropriate living trust for a married couple can minimize estate taxes. Once your trust is established, you must "fund" it. This means that all of your assets should be transferred to the name of the trust with you as trustee or if married, you can be co-trustees.

✓ If your primary concern is to reduce estate taxes, control your assets, transfer assets at death and to avoid probate, than a revocable living trust is for you. It holds title (ownership) of assets you put into it, so these assets can avoid probate. You can name an alternative trustee to make sure your assets will be managed and provide for your maintenance should you become disabled or incompetent. You can include your desires such as nursing home, what assets to be sold if that is necessary, and any special needs you might have. A trust can avoid guardianship proceedings when you specify a designated successor trustee to manage and provide for the care of the grantor when the grantor becomes incapacitated or incompetent.

✓ Living trusts are fictional entities holding assets while you are alive. They transfer to the beneficiary immediately upon death without the time and expense of probate. Make sure you put them in the hands of a trustee you can trust if you are disabled and unable to handle your own affairs. The steps in settling a trust are similar to settling an estate. Do this and you will protect the beneficiaries and the assets you want them to receive.

> **HINT:** *A revocable living trust is an entirely private affair. No one, except the beneficiaries at death, needs to know the contents.*

✓ It is possible for a married couple whose combined estates are more than $600,000 to save on Federal estate taxes through a special trust provision in a will or revocable trust. This trust exempts up to

$600,000 from tax in the estate of the first spouse to die and that $600,000 completely bypasses the estate of the second-to-die. The reason for this is the spouse never has the right to control or to bring the assets into the estate. The surviving spouse has income and principal distribution within a defined limit that cannot be exceeded.

The objectives for this type of trust are:
1. It keeps assets out of the estate of the surviving spouse.
2. It still gives the spouse substantial assets to live on.

Example:
If John and Mary have a combined estate of $1,200,000, and their wills leave everything to the survivor of them, there will be no Federal estate tax upon the first death (because of the marital deduction), but the $1,200,000 estate of the survivor will result in Federal estate taxes on the amount over $600,000.

✓ However, if the first of the couple to die leaves $600,000 in trust for the survivor, there is no Federal estate tax because of the "unified credit." The survivor would then have an estate of $600,000 and a trust of $600,000. Upon the death of the second-to-die, the trust of $600,000 is not subject to estate taxes and the $600,000 estate results in the eliminated taxes under the "unified credit." Your attorney can give you the information and set up this trust for you.

- Irrevocable trusts. Also, known as a life-insurance trust:
  ✓ Most people do not know that the proceeds of a life insurance policy, if not given to a beneficiary, goes to the estate. This amount adds to the total of an estate and can be subject to estate taxes. This can be avoided by naming the trust the beneficiary and then it will be handled according to principles you have set out in the trust documents.
  ✓ These policies are often taken out for the second-to-die. When one spouse dies the property goes to the surviving spouse with no tax consequences. When that spouse dies it pays to the next survivors, usually the children, and gives them money for estate taxes etc.
  ✓ When insurance is transferred to a trust this way it takes away all rights of ownership and you forfeit all rights to cash value as well as the right to take out a loan on the policy. This transfer must be made at least three years before death or the proceeds will be included in your estate.
- Testamentary Trusts — If your will delays the distribution to one or more beneficiaries until they reach a specified age or some other event, your will includes a "testamentary trust." A will with a testamentary trust is not a "simple will." And the preparation costs can be similar to those for revocable living trusts. After the will is probated and the administration of the probate estate is complete, the testamentary trust receives the assets allocated to it. The trustee must file an annual accounting to the court and continuing court supervision is required. This results in continuing costs

until the beneficiaries' shares are distributed.
- ◆ Spendthrift trust:
    1. Protects assets from potential spending, divorce and creditors.
    2. Trust can manage and eventually distribute the assets in installments when the children are more mature.
    3. Can be established by will or a trust document during your lifetime.
    4. You can name someone other than your children as trustee.
    5. If the trust allows the use of the assets for education, medical etc., it could be taxed to the parent.
- ◆ Q-tip trust (Qualified-terminal Interest Property Trust)

> **Example** — *Provides for a new present spouse, then on the death of that spouse the assets would go to the children of the first marriage.*

- ✓ Income must be distributed once a year to qualify for the marital deduction of the estate tax to the new spouse.
- ✓ Upon her death, the assets are included in her estate and after the tax liability is disbursed to the children of the previous marriage.
- ◆ Charitable Remainder Trusts (CRT) — is used to gift appreciated assets to a favorite charity but, before these assets are donated to the charity it is set up to provide lifetime or term payments to an individual or to another individual such as a surviving spouse with the remainder going to the

charity. If you decide on this type of trust, check with your attorney as to the pros and cons that could affect you. Remember — once the assets are transferred into a CRT, you cannot take them back. The cost of preparing this type of trust is approximate $1,000.

> *There are a lot of self-help do-it-yourself kits on the market for living trusts. If you decide to go this route be sure you include all your assets into the trust. I remind you that this is not a book to give you legal advice. Contact a competent lawyer. It will be cheaper in the long run. If you do not specifically include assets and your wishes in the trust, then they will pass by will or without a will, by statute. Either way it will take a probate procedure before your heirs will receive the assets.*

The idea that trusts avoid estate taxes is wrong. Most trusts are not set up for that purpose. There are definitely some advantages in setting up a trust including:

1. Privacy. The contents of a trust do not become part of the public record
2. Property in the trust pass to the beneficiary at date of death with the income from that day taxable to the beneficiary.
3. Volatile assets needing constant attention will not be delayed during a probate process.
4. You have a contingency plan in the event of your incapacity.
5. Avoid the fees of probate.

CHAPTER 14

✳

WILLS AND LIVING WILLS

WILLS AND LIVING WILLS

Everyone should have a will. It allows any assets, whether the amount is large or small, to pass to the people you choose. A will plays a major role in your estate planning and eliminates many of the problems for your survivors.

Dying without a will can be the biggest mistake you make. If you have substantial assets, minor children, or any property that cannot be passed to your survivors by other means, it is essential. A will is necessary to cover your finances, wishes, and heirs you want to receive the benefits. But, dying without discussing and making plans with your spouse may be a worse mistake. Issues must be addressed that affect both of you when, not if, one of you is left alone.

When one of you dies, does the retirement stop, what happens to a business, where are the records of accounts, where are the deeds and titles, can the survivor afford to maintain the home, will the survivor be able to find the necessary documents, does the spouse know the wishes about final internment, etc.? Each of these issues should be discussed and resolved between the two of you. You both have different needs and your wills and estate plans should encompass all of these needs.

While it is true that most of the time, the husband is the breadwinner, this gender bias does not always fall

WILLS AND LIVING WILLS

true. You may be living on two incomes now to make ends meet. The surviving spouse in all probability will need all of the money and assets to live on in the future. A will can:

- ◆ Protect your husband or wife. Most people assume that when property is held jointly it will naturally go to the survivor but, the state laws vary and a percentage can go to the children. If you are married and want your spouse to own everything after your death, it is usually a good idea to have a will that plainly says that and avoid any possible confusion later.
- ◆ Distribute your assets to the recipients of your choice.
- ◆ Allow you to close the books on all your earthly possessions and responsibilities the way you choose.
- ◆ Ensure that your desires are fulfilled.
- ◆ Provide you with peace of mind in the knowledge that your temporal affairs are taken care of.
- ◆ Conserve your assets and reduce the administrative costs of probate.
- ◆ Allow you to affirm your basic beliefs with your favorite charitable organizations.

WHAT IS A WILL?

- ◆ A will is your formal legal declaration passing your assets at the time of your death. It is a document that directs the administration and distribution of your estate. A will covers all assets held in your name at time of death that do not pass by trust, beneficiary or right of survivorship. Everyone should have a current will. If you do not have a

will at this time, **do it.** Get yourself a competent attorney and make sure to include all your wishes.
- ◆ It should be in writing and signed and witnessed. Each state has different requirements, so check with your state statutes. In some states a handwritten will is valid, in some the will can be oral, while in others the will must be typewritten. In some states an "out of state" will is not valid. (Check your state estate and probate laws.)
- ◆ You must be of competent mind and memory. This means you are aware of what you are doing and have "the capacity" to sign a legal document. Also, you must be of legal age for your state.
- ◆ A current will can take advantage of both Federal and state estate tax deductions and/or exclusions.
- ◆ Having a current, up to date will ensures that your estate is administered with minimum delay, expense and intervention by the courts.

Common Mistakes:
1. Procastinating — putting off until tomorrow getting your affairs in order — when there is not a deadline to death.
2. Get it done and over with — doing estate planing in haste before traveling or before an emergency is usually too emotional and rushed.
3. Dying without a will, a living will, or any plan of extended health care — this might be OK if there are no children, no spouse, no family, no nothing.
4. Not retitling everything to coordinate with your plan — joint ownership into single ownership or visa-versa, including a trust name, insurance beneficiaries, etc.

Wills and Living Wills

5. Not updating your final papers — changing home states, change in family members, second marriages, etc.
6. Not naming an executor and/or an alternate.
7. Making sure the executor is a well-organized person and obtaining his consent.
8. Using forms without understanding the wording and the final consequences.
9. Letting your family scramble to find your papers and/or documents.

With a Will
1. You decide who receives a share of your assets.
2. You decide how and when your beneficiaries receive their inheritance.
3. You decide who manages your estate (executor, trustees, etc.).
4. You reduce estate taxes and administrative expenses.
5. You select a guardian for your child.
6. You can appoint a trustee to take care of the property and finances the child inherits.
7. You provide for the orderly continuance or sale of a family business and investments.

Without a Will
1. State law will determine who inherits your assets-they could pass to an unfriendly relative.
2. The terms and timing are set by law. Your children could be left with unlimited control of a sizable estate.
3. The Court will appoint an administrator, at your estate's expense, whose ideas may not be compatible with your own.
4. Administrative expenses and unnecessary taxes can excessively deplete your estate.
5. The Court will appoint a guardian for your child and the money until the age of 18.
6. Financial loss and family hardships may result from untimely court-ordered sales.

Besides these mistakes, stop your excuses and answer these questions:
1. Everybody knows what they will get when I die. Do they? Will your daughter want grandma's vase or will your son fight for it?

2. Who will get which investment?
3. I am not old enough to think about a will yet. What age is old enough? How do you know what will happen this afternoon, tomorrow or the day after?
4. My brother will take care of my kids. Have you asked him? If he does take care of them, how will he support them? Does his wife agree?
5. It costs too much. Do you have any idea the cost of probate without a will? Are you willing to leave that expense and the loss of assets up to the courts? A simple will should cost no more than $100.
6. Who is going to pay my bills?

If you do not have a current will, then not only will the state government take over the distribution by law, the attorneys will get their fair share. (or more) In most states the widow/er will receive a third to one-half of the estate with the children getting the balance. Many spouses cannot live on the portion they receive and are forced to sell their home or other assets just to survive.

> **Hint:** *Take time to list all assets and liabilities as well as their location. Make sure your family knows of the list and where you keep the list.*
>
> *Think about the executor you name to be sure it is someone you trust to make certain the beneficiaries are protected.*

INTESTATE SUCCESSION:
If you die without a will or trust, the state you live in has a statutory (law) plan for distribution of your

WILLS AND LIVING WILLS

assets. There are many problems with this situation:
- ◆ The statutory distribution may not be according to your wishes.
- ◆ Your estate will be subject to probate fees and costs along with the time delay it takes for a probate proceeding.
- ◆ If you have an estate in excess of $600,000 it will be subject to estate taxes, which might have been avoided if you had planned for distribution.
- ◆ For any minor children the court will have to appoint a guardian. This person may or may not be the person you would have chosen.

MOVING:

Anytime you move across state lines the estate laws change. Be sure to review all your estate plans within six months of the move. This is even more vital when moving to or from a community property state. Change your legal domicile, voting registrations and of course, your automobile title.

Each state has different income tax laws as well as estate tax laws that you need to be aware of. Check with the state Department of Revenue for information.

Make out a new will, update any trust you might have and notify your insurance agent to go over car and home policies to see if it they are now all correct for the new state. (Insurance is state regulated and varies dramatically from state to state.) Discounts can vary from one state to another or from one city to another.

SECOND FAMILY WILLS:

Experts say there will be more than one marriage for most of us. Some of this is due to the increased life span after the death of a spouse and some will be due because of the increasing rate of divorce. Whatever the reason, if you want to protect your children of a former marriage, you must plan ahead of time. Ann Landers in her syndicated column told it just the way it is. Here is her column:

Dear Ann Landers: My 65-year-old, widowed father remarried and lived with his new wife, "Greta," for five years until he died. Greta was four years younger that Dad and has seven grown children. They were financial equals when they married.

Dad always told me and my four siblings that we were provided for in his will. When he died, however, we learned from Greta that he had changed his will six months before and left her everything, including a sizable amount of money. Although we were startled by Dad's change of heart, none of us thought it was appropriate to question this or protest.

Now, five years later, Greta is talking about remarrying. My sister wants to know if Greta will provide for us in her will to make certain that Dad's money does not become mingled with the new husband's. She also wants to be sure that Dad's investments are managed wisely.

I am uncomfortable asking Greta about this. I think when Dad changed his will, that was the time to discuss future plans. Since no such discussion took place, I believe we have no business asking Greta to do anything unless she offers.

What do you say, Ann? My siblings and I are all adults and not dependent on this money. If you say it's OK to talk to Greta about this, how should we

bring it up? — Wondering in Washington State
Dear Wondering: *The money your dad left his second wife belongs to her. Whether or not she remarries has no relevance to her inheritance.*
(Permission granted by Ann Landers and Creators Syndicate.)

There were several replies to this letter again brought up in her column. Some of the suggestions covered these points:

- Provisions set in a trust for the income to go to the wife for her lifetime with the remainder going to his children.
- Urging anyone to hire a lawyer to have a trust and/ or will written.
- Possibly contesting the will if it was only written six months before death.
- Actually asking to see the will.
- Setting up a prenuptial before marriage. (See Chapter 23, "Prenuptial Agreements")
- Checking into how property was titled. (Separate names or jointly.)
- Always seeking legal advice when there is substantial property or children involved.

I thank Ann Landers for her making clear what is growing into a major problem for many families. Many married couples immediately put property in joint names. When one of them dies, the full title of that asset immediately goes to the survivor. A will stating differently has no effect on any jointly held property.

Jane and Paul were married last year. Paul changed the title of his home into joint tenancy with his wife, Jane. In plain terms, this means if Paul dies first, Jane will own the home. Any former children or family will not have a claim on that home.

Plan now before a problem or emergency comes up or if incompetency occurs. Seek legal and financial help. Ask questions and do what is right for you.

LIVING WILLS:

This is not to be mistaken for a regular will or a living trust. A living will gives advance directives, in case you are incapacitated, to someone you trust to allow them to make medical decisions for you. It is a signed and witnessed document. It instructs a physician to withhold or withdraw needed intervention from the signer "if" she or he is in a terminal condition and is unable to make a decision about medical treatment. The inability to make a decision is determined by the attending doctor. Many emergency rooms do not recognize a living will. Only a few states now authorize "do not resuscitate orders" only on cardiopulmonary arrest.

Unless living wills and other directives are drawn up properly and you take steps to protect and instigate their provisions, medical personal and providers may ignore them. It is possible to get care just the opposite of what you had intended.

If an emergency comes up, someone will need to locate a relative or close friend. You will need to provide this person with information. Talk to this person and ask for their help if and when it might be needed. No one expects to be called but, if they are, what do you want. Questions will be asked of them, sometimes even before any treatment can be started. In addition, it is a good idea to add the following information for the person that will be called in case of emergency.

- ◆ Bring up the subject with your doctor and ask for any information he can give you.
- ◆ Give both your doctor and your family your feelings about organ donor or life-support systems and fill in a donor card if that is your decision.
- ◆ List the name and telephone number of your personal doctor, medications you are currently taking, allergies, chronic conditions.
- ◆ List the names and telephone numbers of family members, friends, and employer.
- ◆ List your end-of-life feelings and requests.

(AARP Legal Counsel for the Elderly has prepared a booklet called Planning for Incapacity: A Self Help Guide for each state. Order from Legal Counsel for the Elderly/AARP, PO Box 96474, Washington, D.C. 20090-6474 . (Cost $5.00 each)

Last Will and Testament
(Copy this form.)

BE IT KNOWN, that I,_____ of _____, County of_____, in the State of_____, being of sound mind, do make and declare this to be my Last Will and Testament expressly revoking all my prior Wills and Codicils at any time made.

I. **Personal Representative:**
I appoint_____ of_____, as Personal Representative of this my Last Will and Testament and provide if this Personal Representative is unable or unwilling to serve than I appoint _____ of_____, as alternate Personal Representative who shall be authorized to carry out all provisions of this Will and pay my just debts, obligations and funeral expenses. I further provide my Personal Representative shall not be required to post bond in this or any otherjurisdiction and direct that no expert appraisal be made of my estate unless required by law.

II. **GUARDIAN:**
In the event I shall die as the sole parent of minor children, then I appoint_____, as Guardian of said minor children. If this named Guardian is unable or unwilling to serve, then I appoint_____, as alternate Guardian.

III. **BEQUESTS:**
I direct that after payment of all my just debts, my property be bequeathed in the manner following:
   a)
   b)
   c)
   d)

IN WITNESS WHEREOF, I have hereunto set my hand this day of _____, 199___, to this my Last Will and Testament.

Signature _____

WILLS AND LIVING WILLS

IV. WITNESSED:

This Last Will and Testament of_____was signed and declared to be his/her Last Will and Testament in our presence and at his/her request and in the presence of each other, we do hereby witness same on this_____ day of_____, 199___.

Witness Signature   Address

Witness Signature   Address

Witness Signature   Address
State of_____, County of_____.
We,_____,_____,
_____, and_____,
the testator and the witnesses, respectively, whose names are signed to the attached and foregoing instrument, were sworn and declared to the undersigned that the testator signed the instrument as his/her Last Will and Testament and that each of the witnesses, in the presence of the testator and each other, signed the will as witnesses.

Testator: Witness

                             Witness

                             Witness

State of_____County of_____ On_____ Before me,_____, appeared_____, personally known to me (or proved to me on the basis of satisfactory evidence) to be the person(s) whose name(s) is/are subscribed to the within instrument and acknowledged to me that he/she/they executed the same in his/her/their authorized capacity(ies), and that by his/her/their signature(s) on the instrument the person(s), or the entity upon behalf of which the person(s) acted, executed the instrument.

Signature   Affiant_____ Known___ Produced ID
                     Type of ID
                                          (Seal)

Before using this form, read it and make any changes for your situation. Consult with an attorney if you have any questions.

Living Will Declaration
(Copy this form.)

I hereby make this declaration of the ___ Day of _____, 199_.

I, _____, being an adult of sound mind and emotionally and mentally competent to make this declaration, willfully and voluntarily make known my desires that my death shall not be artificially postponed, and hereby declare:

If at any time I should be diagnosed by at least two (2) physicians who have personally examined me, one of whom shall be my attending physician, as having an incurable and irreversible injury, disease, or illness, and that my death is imminent, where the application of life-sustaining procedures would serve only to artificially prolong the moment of my death, I direct that such procedures be withheld or withdrawn, and that I be permitted to die naturally, with only the administration of medication, food or fluids or the performance of medical procedures deemed necessary to alleviate suffering and provide comfort and care.

In the absence of my ability to give directions regarding the use of such life-sustaining and prolonging procedures, it is my intention that this declaration shall be honored by my family and physicians as the final expression of my legal right to refuse medical or surgical treatment, and I accept the consequences of such refusal.

If I have been diagnosed as pregnant and that diagnosis is known to my attending physician, this directive shall be without force or effect during the term of my pregnancy.

I, my estate, and my heirs and successors will hold harmless any person, organization, or institution from any and all liability that may be incurred as a result of following the instructions set forth and contained in this declaration.

This declaration shall remain in effect unless and until it is revoked by me. I understand that I may revoke this declaration at anytime. This declaration shall be governed by the laws of the state.

Signature and date
City_____ County_____ State___ of Residence.

CHAPTER 15

※

FINAL ARRANGEMENTS

FINAL ARRANGEMENTS

Even if you are uncomfortable about the subject of death, don't be tempted to leave the details of final arrangements to those who survive. Let your family know what you want. It will save them agonizing hours trying to make decisions. Share your thoughts and wishes with them. Advance planning can help ensure that costs will be controlled, or at the least, kept to a minimum.

Preparation can make all the problems easier. I advise and urge you to put together all your estate planning documents. Put them in a safe location and, **please**, tell someone where to find them.

Don't forget the importance of a memorial service. A memorial ceremony is held to honor someone who has died and to give closure to those left behind. The truth is, we take comfort in attending a ceremony especially if it reflects the wishes and personality of the person we cared about.

Choosing a funeral director is vital from a financial point of view. You can choose the type of burial and the funeral arrangements based on what you want to spend. Mortuaries can collect the body from the place of death, prepare the body, store the body, make the arrangements with the cemetery, conduct the service and make transportation arrangements. Give your survivors a chance to say goodby with a minimum of cost and anguish.

Final Arrangements

The person you named as your Personal Representative should retain an attorney (not necessarily the one you used) experienced in estate and probate laws. This attorney will guide the representative through the funeral and legal process and also help in the gathering and distribution of your assets. The attorney can tell your Personal Representative which of the bills you are liable for and which ones not to pay.

PRE-FUNERAL ARRANGEMENTS:
- Select the funeral home or mortuary and check their present and pre-arrangement plans. Discuss with them what you want and the terms of pre-payment or payment. Be sure to read very carefully all documents. Ask what the options are if you change your mind and no longer want to deal with them and/or if you move to a different part of the country. Is there any refund of the money?
- Select the type of burial. This includes the way you want your body to be treated (embalmed or cremation). You can even choose a casket or urn.
- Select the type of service to fit your wishes. There is usually more than one service and it can be set anywhere you choose. Do you want an open viewing or have you something else in mind? List the music that is important to you and the person to officiate at the service. Prepare a list of possible pallbearers. Anything you are able to give your survivors will make it easier for whomever is caring out your wishes.
- Cremation plans can be made. Check for plans through your local Cremation Society.
- Select the place for your remains and how you will

be transported. This could be a local cemetery, a family plot in another part of the country or a mausoleum. You can talk about the type of marker and/or inscription (epitaph).
- **Make sure your family knows your wishes.**

IMMEDIATE FUNERAL ARRANGEMENTS by Personal Representative or family:
- Documents needed — will, Social Security number, birth certificate, military discharge, marriage license, Veterans Administration number, cemetery and/or cremation papers.
- Death near residence — usually funeral director can make all the necessary arrangements.
- Death in another part of United States — the local funeral director will prepare remains for shipment to the funeral director near your residence or place of burial. Transportation of the remains must be paid by the survivors. (There are exceptions for military or veterans.)

> **HINT:** *Remains must not be shipped until notification of acceptance by place of internment.*

- Death in a foreign country — call the American Embassy immediately for information and follow their advice.
- Select a funeral director with whom you will be able to work. Sit down with the director and let him help you make the final arrangements. Ask him about alternatives and be sure to ask about prices before you sign anything. Check with him

Final Arrangements

to make sure the price includes what you want and that you will not be billed for something later.
◆ Select the final resting place if this has not been done by the deceased.
◆ Make arrangements for any services and/or viewings. This includes who will perform the service (minister, rabbi, service organization, military, etc.) as well as music and pallbearers.
◆ Decide on the memorial program for the service.
◆ Order flowers and give the funeral director information on any charity memorial.
◆ Check with your local newspaper on their policy for obituaries. Each paper has different rules and charges.
◆ Make arrangements now for several copies of the death certificate. These can be obtained from the funeral director or the health department. You will need a certified death certificate for all places you need to change name or title.
◆ If military, ask about a flag for the casket.

SOURCES OF IMMEDIATE FUNDS:
◆ Funds in joint accounts where the survivor has access. (Check your state laws on this.)
◆ Funds in the survivors name.
◆ Payment of life insurance where survivor is the beneficiary. (Takes about two weeks.)
◆ Paychecks and/or other benefit from the employer.

NOTIFY:
◆ Your attorney of record. He/she might have the original of the will and you will need to file this with the court.

- The employer and/or pension holder. Find out about all benefits to which you are entitled.
- Social Security Administration if drawing benefits.
- Appropriate military service agency (VA, reserve military group, military service)
- Life insurance companies. (Ask for forms for payment of claims.)
- Banks, brokers, credit unions, etc.
- Professional and Fraternal Organizations.

BURIAL BENEFITS:
- Social Security's current death benefit is $250. (SSA Form-8, Application for lump-Sum)*
- Veterans Administration current burial allowance is $250 in a national cemetery or $150 if buried elsewhere. (VA Form 21-530, Application for burial benefits)*
- Check with the deceased employer or payer of a pension for any benefits available.

*Forms must be filled out within two years of date of the death.

> HINT: It is easier to order several death certificates immediately from the funeral director. Determine out how many you will need and then order a couple of extras.

SURVIVOR BENEFITS:
- Employer — Check with any current or past employer and get all the information about pension, savings, medical and life insurance plans. (Ask for a booklet on benefits.)
- Civil Service Retirement System — Ask for an **Application for Death Benefits.**

FINAL ARRANGEMENTS

- U.S. Government — *Claim for Unpaid Compensation of Deceased Civilian Employee,* standard form 1153)
- Retired — Write to any pension payer or place of retirement for survivor benefits.
- Life insurance — Write or call each company and request the benefit form and inquire about what information will be required.
- Retirement plans — Write each plan requesting the information and the forms needed for transfer of funds or for payout.
- Check your records for any IRA, SEP, Keogh, 401(k), or any other plan and make arrangements for transfer of funds or for payout.
- Social Security — If you are a widow(er) or minor, check for benefits. The average funeral costs more than $4,500. Social Security pays those who qualify only $250 toward the final expenses.

> **HINT:** *Remember some employers and credit cards carry accident and life insurance benefits.*

EXECUTOR AND/OR SURVIVOR:
- First duty is to bring together and list all assets of the estate.
- List all assets that pass outside of the estate. (Insurance that goes directly to beneficiaries, jointly owned property, bank accounts, trusts, etc.)
- If there is property to transfer, contact the attorney to begin the probate process.
- Check for all debts of the deceased. List them as to categories such as expenses, medical, debts, fu-

neral, credit cards, etc.
- ◆ Cancel and/or change ownership and list those changes that need to be made:
  - → Credit cards
  - → Utility listings
  - → Bank accounts and CD's
  - → Ownership of securities, Government bonds
  - → Real estate (including home)
  - → Military ID
  - → Safety deposit boxes
  - → Automobile, home and other insurance policies
  - → Memberships or subscriptions

RECORDS: (See Chapter 2 "Records")
- ◆ Pay all bills by check and keep the receipts.
- ◆ Use duplicate deposit slips and indicate on the copies the origin of the money.
- ◆ Keep all the tax records, any Federal or state estimated payment, last pay stub, real estate, intangible tax, etc.
- ◆ Do a financial inventory (or financial statement) to help you work through the maize of finances. (See Chapter 3 "Financial Statements")
- ◆ Make an inventory of the home, all collectibles, securities etc. Take photographs for a record.
- ◆ Appraise any property, if necessary, both real and personal.
- ◆ Maintain a file with copies of all probate papers.

VETERAN'S AFFAIRS:
Any veteran who served on active duty and was honorably discharged is usually eligible to be buried in a national cemetery. Check with the local Veteran's

Administration for qualification or call 800-827-1000.

The American Bar Association has a book available entitled, *The American Bar Association Guide to Wills and Estates*. Other books available are *How to Plan Your 'Total' Estate With a Will and Living Will Without the Lawyer's Fees* by Benji O. Anosike, and *Your Living Trust and Estate Plans: How To Maximize Your Family's Assets and Protect Your Loved Ones* by Harvey J. Platt.

Funeral and Burial Instructions
(Copy this form.)

I,_____, hereby designate and direct that upon my death my remains be disposed or as follows:
1. It is my wish to be buried in _(Place)_ , _(County)_ , _(State)_ . (Section #___, Plot #___) The deed to this plot is with the original of these funeral instructions. (If a plot has been bought.)
2. (If applicable) It is my wish that my remains be cremated at_____ And that my ashes are disposed of in accordance with the desires of my next of kin or by the enclosed instructions.
3. It is my wish that my funeral service and/or memorial service be conducted at_____. It is also my wish that the following arrangements for my funeral/memorial service be honored:
    a. Conducted by —
    b. Music —
    c. Other —

The fully executed original of my last will and testament and my living trust can be found in_____.

Signature and date _____

Estate Planning Records
(Copy this form.)

- ❑ Current Will
- ❑ Trust Documents
- ❑ Birth Certificate
- ❑ Marriage Certificate
- ❑ Military Discharge
- ❑ Social Security Number
- ❑ Medicare Number
- ❑ Funeral and Burial Instructions
- ❑ Prepaid Funeral Plans
- ❑ Mortuary or Funeral Home
- ❑ Cemetery Deed or Location
- ❑ Personal Choice of Service
- ❑ Location or type of Immediate Funds
- ❑ Life Insurance Policies
- ❑ Employer Benefit Booklet
- ❑ Pension Booklet

CHAPTER 16

✳

PROBATE

PROBATE

Probate is the legal process of winding down and wrapping up of all the financial affairs of a deceased person, determining the successors, and passing the assets to the survivors and/or beneficiaries. Generally probate has four different segments:
1. Collect and inventory the assets.
2. Contact all creditors and pay all the debts.
3. File and pay all taxes due.
4. Distribute the balance to the heirs or beneficiaries.

The legal process has two aspects that are sometimes confused. First, it is the process of proving the document is the last will and testament of the deceased. Second, it is the process of administering the estate. Probate also is the "admitting the will to probate." To admit a will to probate means that a probate judge has determined that the document is the last will of the deceased and the assets (property) should be distributed according to the will.

WHAT ARE CONSIDERED PROBATE ASSETS?

Generally, probate assets are those assets in the deceased's sole name at death and owned solely by the person, and which have no provisions for automatic succession of ownership at death.

◆ A bank account or investment account in the sole

name of the deceased person.
- ◆ Life insurance without a current beneficiary is payable to the estate.
- ◆ Real estate, other than the homestead, titled in the sole name of the deceased.
- ◆ This is not a complete list. Check state laws and an attorney for more information.

WHAT ARE NOT CONSIDERED PROBATE ASSETS?

Any asset that does not pass under the will is a non-probate asset. It can include:
- ◆ Real property with titles in "joint tenancy with rights of survivorship" or "tenancy by the entireties." (Tenancy by the entireties is void after a divorce is final.)
- ◆ Personal property such as a bank account in joint names or if the account is held in the name of a trust.
- ◆ Property held in a living (revocable) trust. This can include home, automobiles, stocks, bonds, etc.
- ◆ Insurance policy benefits with a current beneficiary.
- ◆ Retirement plans with current beneficiaries.

> **HINT:** *Non-probate assets should be carefully coordinated with the current will.*

WHO GETS THE ASSETS IF THERE IS NO WILL?

If you die "intestate," it is called dying without a will. Each state is different and you must check the laws. There are legal provisions that are subject to certain exceptions for homestead property, exempt personal

property, and any statutory allowance to a surviving spouse and lineal descendants the decedent was obliged to support. Generally the heirs are as follows:
- ◆ Surviving spouse and no lineal descendants: The surviving spouse gets everything if there are no lineal descendants.
- ◆ Surviving spouse and lineal descendants: Each state has percentages or an amount that goes to the spouse and then the balance is shared by the lineal descendants.
- ◆ No Surviving spouse, but lineal descendants: If there was not a spouse then the lineal descendants share the estate. The estate is broken into shares with a diseased child's share going to the descendants of that child.
- ◆ No Surviving spouse and no lineal descendants: If there are none of these surviving the deceased than the surviving parents, and if none, then to the brothers and sisters. If none of these survive, than the law has further disposition provisions.

WHO IS INVOLVED IN THE PROBATE PROCESS?
- ◆ Clerk of the Court of your local jurisdiction: Probate papers are filed with the Clerk of the Court for the county where the decedent lived. A filing fee must be paid before the process can start and be administrated. The clerk will then issue a court file number.
- ◆ Judge acting through your local court system: A Judge will be assigned to the file and preside over all the probate proceedings. The judge approves or appoints a Personal Representative and issues the "letters of administration" giving authority to

this person to act on behalf of the estate. He will also hold hearings, resolve questions and enter written orders as necessary.
◆ Attorney to act for the Personal Representative: In almost all cases the Personal Representative must be represented by an attorney. If the entire estate goes to one beneficiary, it may not be necessary. The attorney advises the Personal Representative on the rights and duties under the law and represents him in estate proceedings. A will mandating that a particular attorney be employed is not binding on the Personal Representative.

> **HINT:** *The attorney does not represent the beneficiaries of the estate.*

◆ Personal Representative: The Personal Representative is the person, trust or bank appointed by the court to administer the estate of a deceased. Sometimes the word "Personal Representative" is replaced by executor, executrix, administrator or administratrix. The court directs the Personal Representative to administer the estate according to laws of the state and must:
   1. Gather, identify and safeguard all probate assets.
   2. Publish in the local newspaper a "Notice of Administration" giving notice of the estate and the requirements to file claims and any other papers relating to the estate.
   3. Conduct a conscientious search for creditors and notify them to file claims.
   4. Review claims and object to improper ones

as well as defend any suits brought on such claims.
5. Pay all the valid claims.
6. Hire any necessary professional to assist with the estate.
7. File all necessary tax returns.
8. Pay any gift or estate taxes due from the estate.
9. Pay the administrative expense. (Attorney, Personal Representative, etc.)
10. Distribute any statutory amounts or assets to the surviving spouse and/or family.
11. Distribute the balance of the assets to the heirs.
12. Close the probate estate through the court.

◆ Internal Revenue Service for the filing of personal and estate taxes: A death triggers two actions with the IRS as well as with the state where the deceased lived. It ends the decedent's last tax year and it establishes a new tax entity, the "estate." The Personal Representative may be required to file the following returns depending on the income of the person and the income and size of the estate: (See Chapter 21 "Taxes")
1. Final form 1040 Federal personal income tax return.
2. One or more Form 1041 Federal income tax return for the estate.
3. Final Form 709 Federal gift tax return.
4. Form 706 Federal estate tax return.
5. Check your state revenue office for the filing of personal and estate taxes or contact the local state revenue office for the filing

requirements of the state where the deceased lived.

> **HINT:** *Additionally, the Personal Representative may be required to file other returns as well as dealing with prior tax years.*

WHO CAN BE A PERSONAL REPRESENTATIVE?
- ◆ The Personal Representative can be an individual, attorney, trust or a bank, subject to the restrictions of each state.
- ◆ If the decedent left a valid will, the designated Personal Representative nominated in the will is given preference to serve.
- ◆ If the deceased did not leave a will, the surviving spouse has preference, with second preference to the person selected by a majority of the heirs.

WHAT IS THE BASIC PROCEDURE FOR PROBATE?
- ◆ Open up the probate proceedings.
  1. Retain an attorney to represent the estate.
  2. File the death certificate.
  3. File the current will.
  4. File for and receive "letters of administration."
- ◆ Personal Representative is appointed.
- ◆ Publish "Notice of Administration."
- ◆ Locate and serve notice to all heirs and/or beneficiaries.
- ◆ Review, pay or object to claims.
- ◆ File and pay all taxes due.
- ◆ Pay all expenses of the estate.
- ◆ File the final accounting.

◆ Close the estate.

While this is just a run down of the estate process, there can be many variations. Each estate is different, just as any person is different. In order to save your survivors many of the hassles and time constraints of the probate process, it is important to do some estate planning early. (See Chapter 13 "Estate Planning")

> **HINT:** *The probate lawyers know that if you do not plan ahead and pay them to draw up wills, trusts, etc, they will be paid much more later for probate.*

CHAPTER
17

*

DIVORCE

DIVORCE

The time has come! Somewhere in the back of your mind you have discovered it's not the story book marriage you dreamed of. In fact, it's not even a way of life that you want to continue. No matter what the reasons, you have decided something is happening, and you need to make some preparations to protect yourself.

If you are not in physical danger, play it cool — don't overreact. Start immediately to look out for your own best interests. It's your future and what you do now will have a lasting effect. Don't talk about divorce or separation until you are ready and have prepared a plan. Do not sign or agree to **anything** without a legal consultation. **Know your rights and don't be intimidated!**

> **HINT:** *Remember the best defense is a strong offense. Now is the time to make your basic preparation and decisions.*

This is one of the most emotional times of your life. This is the time to control your emotions and to think ahead. Divorce is treated by the legal system as simply a financial dissolution of a commercial partnership. If you were terminating a business, you would plan ahead and expect your fair share. You must do the same in a

Divorce

divorce situation. You have to fight to get your fair share or you will lose. Educate yourself on the divorce possibilities in the court system, the laws, and the facts.

- ◆ Protect your immediate and future safety and that of your children. Know who to contact if abuse of **any** sort is threatened. Keep the telephone number in your wallet for emergencies. Stay in touch with a close and supportive friend or relative.
- ◆ Start by collecting and copying all records you can find. Take the copies and put them in a safe place. (See Chapter 2 "Records")
- ◆ If there are credit cards in joint names, have the company issue one in your name. Take your name off the joint accounts. **You must write to them** saying that you will no longer be responsible for purchases made by your spouse after that date.
- ◆ Money in savings and checking accounts may disappear rapidly and completely the minute divorce is mentioned. Either take it out if your name is on the account or notify the bank that nothing is to be withdrawn without **both** signatures. Remember, you will need money to live on during the divorce proceedings and money to pay your attorney.
- ◆ Cash from current "Home Equity" loans is available to either of you with only one signature. If **one** spouse takes it all out, **both** spouses are liable to pay it back. The same holds true for credit lines.
- ◆ Open a separate bank or savings account at another institution. This will give you some money in reserve for living expenses and for legal fees.
- ◆ Contact a Divorce Financial Consultant as soon as you anticipate a divorce situation. This person will help you prepare, and analyze financial informa-

tion. Be prepared before you see the attorney. It will save hours of legal fees and make it easier to get the process started.
- ◆ You can seek the advice of an attorney without retaining him/her. This will give you information as to your immediate rights.
- ◆ Remain in your home if at all possible. Don't let the other person force you out, unless you or your children are in danger. Courts tend to award the home to the person living in the residence.
- ◆ If you are having trouble with your mail being intercepted or taken, rent a post office box in your name only. Change addresses to the box for important mail.
- ◆ Watch what you say to others. It will be passed on and may give you trouble later. Try not to put your joint friends in the middle where they must choose sides. You may get back together, and then everyone will be uncomfortable.
- ◆ Keep a concealed diary of important occurrences. Note financial, social, and business dealings.

Look before you leap. Don't give out any personal information such as your Social Security number, bank references, financial condition, credit card numbers, etc. over the phone. When divorce is in the picture, even reputable people will call for information. Everything you have copied or discovered should be put in a safe place outside the home, perhaps in a lock box at your **new** bank.

> **HINT:** *Educate yourself and fight for your rights.*

GENERAL DIVORCE PROCEDURE

As soon as you retain an attorney for a divorce, you enter the legal system and the procedure has started. Your attorney will discuss with you the pros and cons of the different ways your case can be handled. A good attorney will try hard to work out a settlement before it comes to all out war in the courtroom. I am going to assume no settlement could be reached, and that you will have to go through all the steps necessary to obtain a final judgment of divorce.

- ◆ The formal start of a divorce proceeding begins when one of the parties' attorney files a "Petition for Dissolution." In some states this is called a petition, and in others it is called a complaint. It must be filed with the Clerk of the Court of your county and will contain basic information about date of marriage, residency, jurisdiction of the court, the allegations, and the remedies. This is a legal document called a pleading which tells the court why you are there and asks for all the relief or action you want from the court.

> **HINT:** *The party initiating the divorce is the Petitioner. The party receiving the petition is the Respondent.*

- ◆ After the petition is filed, the Clerk of the Court will issue a summons to be served on the other spouse along with a copy of the initial petition. Service must be completed for the court to have legal jurisdiction over the Respondent.
- ◆ The Respondent usually has twenty (20) days to answer in one of the following ways:

- a) He can file a counter-petition.
- b) He can answer and not contest the petition.
- c) He can do nothing and the Petitioner will get a divorce through default.

◆ As soon as the initial petition is filed, a temporary hearing may be held. It can include motions for support or maintenance during the divorce process. It might also include a restraining order, an injunction forbidding disposal of property, visitation rights, medical coverage, etc.

◆ During the course of a contested divorce, there will be "motions" made to the court from both parties asking for different actions. It can include contempt and failure to pay ordered support. It can also include motions to force compliance to discovery, allow or not allow visitation with the children, etc.

◆ If necessary, the Petitioner will answer the counterclaim. Then the discovery process begins. This can include one or many of the following ways for either party to find out necessary facts and to get documents from the other party.
- a) Interrogatories: written questions for the other party to answer and sign under oath.
- b) Production: documents produced for and/or copying by the other party.
- c) Deposition: oral questions of one of the parties or a third person under oath.
- d) Subpoena: issued by the Clerk of the Court to any person to answer or produce information. Also, a subpoena is used to compel a witness to testify.
- e) Appraisals: used to find the fair market value of an asset.

- f) Child custody consultations: psychologists, classes for divorcing parents, HRS, etc.
- g) Mediation: usually used to try to settle distribution of marital property, but it also is used as an informal discovery tool by some attorneys to get information from the opposing party.

◆ All during this period of time the attorneys should be going through the process of settling the division of marital assets and liabilities. They will be calling and writing to each other with offers and counteroffer.

◆ Before the final hearing the judge may call a "pretrial" hearing. At this hearing the attorneys will go over the facts of the case. Any facts they can agree to will be noted and will not be reargued in court. It gives the judge a preview of the case.

◆ In some states a final divorce hearing is held in front of a hearing officer. In others it will be before a judge. Sometimes it is held in the judge's chambers and at other times in an open court.

Each attorney will present his side of the case. You will sit at one side of a table with your attorney next to you. After you have been sworn in, testimony will be given by you and/or your spouse. There may be experts called to verify value of assets or medical problems. Then each attorney will have time to sum up the facts to the judge and to ask for the relief wanted.

◆ The final judgment is the order made by the judge. He may do this immediately or he may take all the evidence into consideration and rule later. He also can rule on some of the issues and take other issues into consideration for later ruling. Either way the decision by the judge will be based on the facts and the state laws applicable.

HINT: Keep copies of all papers received or sent to your attorney or to the Clerk of the Court. File them in order so you can refer to them when necessary.

◆ If you do not agree with the rulings made in the final judgment, you may ask for a rehearing. In most states you have ten (10) days from the date of the order to ask for this. The judges very rarely grant a rehearing unless you can show an error on the part of the court or a great wrong being done, such as lack of evidence or wrong evidence presented, perjury, etc.

◆ If you still do not agree with the order, you may appeal to the next higher court. Be forewarned that any appeal will cost more in legal fees and costs. Get legal advice on the issues from a different attorney before you go to this expense.

◆ Enforcement of the "Final Judgment" is the next step, and again it will cost more in legal fees and costs. If one party does not comply with the terms of the order, then you must ask the court for enforcement.

States differ regarding how a divorce can be obtained and the procedure to follow. You are required generally to initiate action in the state and county where one of you maintains a permanent home. Check your local state statutes on this.

DIVORCE

Biographical Information
(Copy this form.)

Name _____ Date of Birth _____

Address _____ Soc. Sec.# _____

_____ Home tel.# _____

_____ Work tel.# _____

Employer _____ Years employed _____

Education _____

Spouse _____ Date of Birth _____

Address _____ Soc. Sec. # _____

_____ Home tel. # _____

_____ Work tel. # _____

Education _____

Attorney _____

Financial advisor _____

Bank _____

Other Financial Institutions _____

Children: (Include grown children)

Name   Age   Residence
_____
_____
_____
_____

Suddenly Alone

CHAPTER
18

✳

COOKIE JAR MONEY

EVERYONE NEEDS COOKIE JAR MONEY

Our mothers had their egg money stored in the cookie jar. Some called it their egg money. Our fathers had a little tucked into their wallets. What happened to that old practice?

Emergencies come up at the most inconvenient times. Yesterday, a friend of mine had his car towed to an impound garage. It was Saturday night, the banks were closed and they wanted cash in the amount of $185. He didn't have cash available until Monday, which meant they kept his car for two more days at $15 per day. This is a small emergency but, to some of you it may be impossible to meet this amount immediately. What are you going to do if the amount is greater?

Now, with no-fault divorce becoming the in-thing, wives, and sometimes husbands, are left without a penny to buy food or even to pay for a place to live. It is vital for everyone whether single or married to have some money they can call their own in case of an emergency. Death and divorce are emergencies. They come without warning. Plans made by one spouse without the other spouse knowing, can tie up cash or other types of accounts, until some legal action is taken by either of the parties. There might not be any ready money avail-

Everyone Needs Cookie Jar Money

able when it is so vitally needed. Take time now and plan to have money put aside in case of an individual emergency.

Without the cookie jar money, how do you buy food or any of the essentials to tide you over. Don't ever believe it won't happen to you. It can and it does! Let's take the following scenario:

Jenny and Paul

Jenny and Paul have been married for thirteen years. They have two children, a home with a mortgage, two cars (a good one that Paul drives and the old van that Jenny drives), some credit card debt, very little savings and Paul has a small IRA. One day Paul comes home from work and states, "I am moving out and I am going to get a divorce."

He also tells her he has closed all the bank accounts, taken her name off all the credit cards, and wants to put the house up for sale. She is stunned. There had been no warning. He leaves and she is left with the house, the children, the old van, and about $22 in her pocket.

This happens every day throughout the country. Not only can Jenny not put food on the table, Paul says he won't give her any money.

She requires legal help and court time to get child support and/or temporary maintenance. She can't hire an attorney without cash. Welfare might help a little, but not for legal fees. The house could fall into foreclosure, the van might be repossessed, good credit can be ruined, etc.

Barbara and Dennis

Dennis went to work one morning feeling fine. All of a sudden, while he was walking down the hall, he slumped and fell to the floor. They rushed him to the hospital, but he was dead before he arrived. Barbara was left alone without any information on what to do. She had never handled the money. She didn't know where the money was or how much was be available.

There were immediate expenses and all the money was tied up in Dennis's name. She had no bank accounts in her name. Even the obituary in the paper required prepayment.

Think ahead now!
You need cookie jar money.

CHAPTER 19

※

MEDICAL AND HEALTH

MEDICAL AND HEALTH

The key to keeping healthy is to be alert and have a greater awareness of the body and the care and exercise it must receive. You need to be aware of any health problems as soon as they occurs and know how and where you can receive the required medical help. You need to be alert to the preventive health services available and the need to take advantage of them. Evidence shows that the influence and choice of a doctor makes a difference in the health and services you receive. Choose carefully. It's your life.

BASIC HEALTH INSURANCE:

When buying insurance you address the amount and type of insurance you will need. The first step is to determine how much coverage you need and how much you can afford to pay. Once you have that in mind, the next step is to check with several insurance companies about offers and incentives that are available to reduce your premium.

There are two traditional health coverages offered by health insurance companies:
- ◆ Basic plan — generally covers doctor's bills, medications, and other medical expenses within certain limits. Some pay for annual physicals and some do not.

MEDICAL AND HEALTH

- Major medical — generally covers extended hospital visits and other medical procedures.

In order to buy medical insurance, a person must fill out an application form outlining past medical history, information on parents, etc. You then pay a premium to bind your application to the insurance company. Any premium or quote you receive will be based on certain factors. They include:

- Amount of risk. Example: A history of high blood pressure or diabetes will mean higher premiums.
- Amount of liability the company has to cover. Example: A history of heart related medical care will mean higher premiums.
- The amount the company has to pay. Example: The higher the co-payment (80/20. 60/40) paid by the insurance carrier, the higher the cost. You can lower your cost by paying the first 20% or 40% of the costs yourself. First dollar coverage is expensive. Also the deductible amount purchased will have a risk factor making the premium higher or lower.
- Company's expenses and investment performance. Example: A company with higher expenses and poor investment will have a higher premium.
- Competition among insurance companies in your community.
- Average medical fees charged by the doctors and hospitals in your community.

Medical insurance companies do not guarantee access to medical care. Some insurance plans do not cover certain services or they require high out-of-pocket expenditures. Read your policy carefully to know what is covered and what is not. Benefits should include doctors' visits, hospital care, preventive care, mental health care, long-term care, prescription drugs, and the full range of reproductive health services. Use the chart at the end of this chapter to compare the costs. Be sure to ask about the percentage paid by the company and what percent or balance will be your responsibility.

> **HINT:** *Before you purchase health insurance, have the agent list the basic benefits and then do your price and benefit comparison.*

MEDIGAP INSURANCE:

When a person reaches age 65 Medicare automatically begins under the Social Security System. Medicare becomes the primary health coverage program. (Some people disabled before the age of 65 may be covered.) Coverage is divided into two parts:

- ◆ Part "A" provides inpatient hospital care, inpatient skilled nursing care, home health care under the supervision of the doctor, and hospice care. All of these are subject to Medicare restrictions. This part is paid for by the Social Security Administration.
- ◆ Part "B" covers doctor's bills and other necessary out-patient medical treatment, therapy and appliances. This part is optional and is paid for by the participant. This fee is deducted each month from Social Security retirement checks.

In order to supplement the amount paid by Medicare, it is vital to purchase what is known as a

"Medigap" policy. Medigap insurance is important for older Americans. These plans cover expenses Medicare does not. Medigap is a co-insurance policy covering part or all of Medicare's deductibles. It increases access to health care for the elderly. Older Americans with Medigap coverage are far likelier than those without additional coverage to be satisfied with their health status and are likely to visit a doctor or hospital facility without delay.

"The sharp increases in Medigap insurance premiums are a threatening prospect for older Americans who are simply trying to make ends meet," said Ron Pollack, executive director of Families USA. "When premiums increase twenty, thirty, and forty percent in one year, many of our nation's elderly are going to be squeezed out of the Medigap market."

LONG TERM CARE INSURANCE:

Long term health care insurance typically is designed to pay some or all of the costs of a nursing home stay when you cannot meet the needs of everyday living on your own. There are policies on the market that cover one or more types of care such as nursing home, adult day care, home health care, etc. Long term policies must meet any and all standards of your State Board of Insurance. Check with your insurance commissioner if you have any questions. Before you purchase a policy ask about the following coverage: (If necessary set up a chart like the one at the end of this chapter for basic insurance covering the different areas.)

- ◆ Skilled nursing care: Includes round the clock medical care by a registered nurse under the supervision of your doctor. Remember, you must be

hospitalized for at least three days prior to admittance into a nursing facility. Medicare will cover some of the costs of your skilled nursing care. Medicare will only cover these in an approved facility. Be sure to ask how this will affect the terms and benefits of the policy.
◆ Intermediate nursing care: This involves daily care supervised by registered nurses and ordered by a physician.
◆ Custodial or personal care: Care for basic needs such as bathing, dressing, eating, toileting, mobility, etc. Skilled medical personal are not needed for this service. The policy costs are much higher if you add this coverage to your policy.
◆ Home health care: The services are provided in a person's home by a licensed home health care agency and supervised by your doctor. Services can include skilled nursing, physical therapy and in some policies cooking, cleaning and errands. If you are homebound, Medicare will pay for home health care for medically necessary services. If Medicare pays, a long-term health policy will not.
◆ Adult day care: This includes programs that provide social and health related services for a group of people. They are licensed by your state.

Policy premiums depend on the type of covered care. Other policies pay only when care is approved in certain types of facilities. Each policy describes and defines the level of care, nature of care and the setting in which the care must be administered. Long term care policies are expensive and might not cover all the expenses you incur. Be careful and shop cautiously for a

MEDICAL AND HEALTH

policy with the benefits you want. Don't duplicate benefits you might have with any other policy. Most companies will not pay if another company has paid. Check the coordination of benefits provision in your policy.

Benefits are only payable when the policyholder cannot perform unaided any two of the activities of daily living: bathing, dressing, eating, transferring, toileting, mobility, etc. or is clinically diagnosed as displaying "impairment of cognitive ability." This determination must come from a licensed practitioner authorized to make this ruling.

Premiums are based on your age on the policy purchase date, the amount of the deductible purchased, any current health problems and the duration and amount of the policy benefits. Keep in mind the safeguards you want and watch out for tricky provisions that can work against you.

> **HINT:** *Read your policy carefully. Make sure you know what is covered and what is not covered.*

Before purchasing a healthcare policy, shop around and ask these questions:
- What type of care is covered and what type of facility is required?
- What is the daily benefit amount and for how long will the daily amount continue?
- When does the policy start paying?
- Is there a maximum amount for each illness or confinement?
- Is there a lifetime maximum?
- Are pre-existing conditions covered and if so, is

there a waiting period?
- Will the premium increase as I get older?
- Does the policy cover mental or nervous conditions?
- Is there inflation protection or can I get increased protection?
- Does the policy cover Alzheimer's disease?
- What happens if I fail to pay a premium?

Finally:
- Don't buy a policy on the agent's first visit.
- Never pay by cash and be sure to get a dated, signed receipt.
- Make your check payable to the insurance company, not the agent.
- Never sign a blank application.

MANAGED HEALTH CARE:

Managed care is on the rise all across the country. New options are now available to lower health care costs. Managed care is a broad approach to health care that aims to lower costs by arranging for care at predetermined or discounted rates, specifying which doctors and hospitals a person can use and overseeing physicians' treatments and services. One of the aspects of this type of health care is toward preventive medicine and an effort to track and coordinate patient treatment. There are two basic types of managed care, Health Maintenance Organizations (HMO's) and Preferred Provider Organizations (PPO's).

1. HMO's (Health Maintenance Organizations) offer complete health care including routine checkups and physical exams. Usually you choose your primary doctor from a list of participating doctors.

MEDICAL AND HEALTH

The primary physician than directs your care to specialists as necessary with all costs except a small visit charge being paid by the HMO.

- ◆ When you have a regular insurance program, you pick the doctor and the facility and your insurer pays for most of the expenses. In an HMO program, the care organization provides or arranges most of your health care and pays for the costs.
- ◆ If you are considering joining an HMO plan, you must look carefully at the options before you decide which is right for you. The type of plan you choose will affect your costs, your choice of doctors and the rules on how and where you may seek medical help. Read the information they provide and see if it will fit your needs.
- ◆ For Medicare recipients there is usually no additional cost to belong to these HMOs. The state pays a fee depending on your locality. If you are interested in these services, call your state insurance commissioner for the ones that service your area.

HINT: *HMOs provide a wide range of health services. Make sure the one you pick is right for you.*

2. PPO's (Preferred Provider Organization) puts the person in charge of their healthcare. When you purchase this type of health care you do not have to decide on the doctors you will use. Instead, you can decide whether to use the PPO each time you

need medical care. If you do use a PPO doctor or hospital, you save money.
- ◆ You will receive a booklet which lists all of the participating doctors' and hospitals' names, addresses, and phone numbers.
- ◆ When you use the PPO, the portion of the medical bills that you usually pay (deductible and coinsurance) are reduced . . . the medical plan pays more of the cost.
- ◆ You usually do not have to pay the deductible for many types of expenses.

POSSIBLE MEDICAL FRAUDS:
- ◆ Long term health insurance: Be aware that there are some companies and agents that prey on consumers. They will try to confuse you, sell you policies that are not beneficial to you or to sell you much more insurance than you need. They are also well known for churning policies. (Exchanging your old policy for a new or different policy so they can earn a bigger first time commission.) It is essential for you to examine and carefully compare prices.
- ◆ Medical quackery: Don't be tempted by fabulous health claims such as "miraculous cure for baldness" "cellulite guaranteed to disappear in days," etc. The real tragedy of health quackery is not the money wasted, but that it may persuade people who are seriously ill to buy useless products rather than seek effective medical treatment. In fact, some of these may actually cause real physical damage or adverse reactions. Watch out for anyone who promises a "quick and painless" cure.

MEDICAL AND HEALTH

- Diet and/or weight: There is no quick and easy solution for weight loss. Weight-loss programs are common in today's society. Unfortunately, some business are unscrupulous and have taken advantage of the image-conscious trend. In recent years a number of health quacks have marketed megavitamins and other pills. They promised the user a perfect body. "Body toning" devices are advertised and sold as substitutes for exercise.

  The weight loss business is a booming industry. It is difficult to sort out all of the competing claims. Some are real, some are misleading and some are just plain false. Remember that any claim that you can lose weight effortlessly is false.

- Health and fitness clubs: Health spas have grown as the lucrative fitness industry gets bigger and bigger. Some of these have closed their doors without a warning to their members while others have never opened after taking the consumers' money for memberships. Some states have enacted legislation for protecting consumers. Check any contract carefully. Read the fine print. (See Chapter 20, "Scams")

SUDDENLY ALONE

Medical Insurance Comparison Chart
(Copy this form.)

BENEFIT	Company #1	Company #2	Company #3
Doctors			
Set Co-payment			
60/40% Payment			
80/20% Payment			
90/10% Payment			
Hospital			
Set Co-payment			
Major Medical ($100,000.00)			
Major Medical ($1,000,000.00)			
Extended Care			
Deductible ($100.00)			
Deductible ($500.00)			
Deductible ($1000.00)			
Prescription Drugs			
Vision Care			
Other			

CHAPTER 20

✳

SCAMS

SCAMS

People alone, especially those suddenly alone, seem to be just the right target for professional schemers. These professionals know people are vulnerable and easily charmed into signing contracts and buying things they not only don't want, but don't need.

You don't necessarily need to be alone to be duped. Watch out for the professional, smooth talking scam artist. Check into their qualifications and don't just buy for the sake of buying.

TELEPHONE SCAMS:

It is hard to tell the honest calls from the dishonest calls. You can refuse to do business with anyone on the phone. It is a good practice to only do business with known companies. Hang up and report to authorities any suspicious sales or solicitation. If it is something that you might be interested in, offer to call back or have them send it to you in writing.

Once you order or answer any telemarketing call, you will be put on what is called a "mooch list." This list is used and sold to others and considered ideal repeat victims. This means that if you are on the **list**. You are likely to be inundated with calls. Beware!

The telephone company can add your name to a list of those refusing solicitation calls. This only protects

SCAMS

you from cold calls, not from someone you have already done business with. Check with your local telephone company for details.

For stopping junk mail you can write to Mail Preference Service, Direct Marketing Association, P.O. Box 9008, Farmingdale, NY 11735-9008. Have them remove your name from most national catalog and other direct mailing lists.

Example #1:

Typical bank scam caper: The gentleman called and said he was from the bank and was investigating forged checks. They needed her help to catch the people forging against her account. He asked her to cash a personal check for $4,000. After cashing the check, she was approached by a gentleman who identified himself as the bank detective. He showed her a badge and took the money to check the serial numbers. He then told her he would take her home to sign some papers and went to get the car. He never came back. ($4,000 gone!)

Example #2:

When a stranger calls and wants to do something for you or give you good news, be wary. Question all motives. Don't send money. (You will never see the money again.) The Department of Justice estimated that senior citizens make up 40-60 percent of the victims in most telemarketing scams. Bogus telemarketing considers the elderly and most particularly widows and widowers easy pickings. These people live alone and welcome talking to someone. If someone calls and asks for money, just hang up. (Money gone!)

Example #3:

One of the latest telephone scams involves getting you to accept charges for a call being made from an outside phone. It is done by someone calling and claiming to be a FCC (Federal Communications Commission) inspector or maybe even representing themselves as an investigator of the long-distance company. Typically, the caller claims to be checking trouble on the consumer's telephone line or equipment. Then the caller says his supervisor will be calling, within a certain time period. He asks that you should just say "yes" when asked to accept charges for that call. Consumers who say "yes" end up allowing their phone numbers to be billed for third-number long-distance calls. (Telephone bill to pay!)

Example #4:

Jane has just received a telephone call saying she had won $10,000 in groceries or a diamond watch. In order to direct deposit the money into her account they needed her checking account number. Later they used that number to take money from her account for purchases as debited amounts. Never give your checking account number to an individual you don't know. Millions of people now are paying bills, buying memberships etc without writing a check. Write

SCAMS

> to your bank immediately to notify you confirming any debit to your account and naming the merchant and listing the withdrawals. (You might be able to get the money back from the bank!)

Eight-hundred numbers are not always free. The Federal government passed a rule that allows companies with toll-free numbers to charge for a specific service or product but, only after the customer gives permission. If the person answering asks you for your telephone number and pin number, it is a tip off that you will be charged for the phone call. Tip: **Don't enter or give any additional digits or codes unless it is your intention to place an order.**

AARP estimates that 14,000 fraudulent telemarketing businesses operate nationwide. They state, "Telemarketing fraud is a crime, and fraudulent telemarketers are criminals." Their research also shows that many of the victims are well-educated, active, financially stable. Linda F. Golodner, president of the National Consumers League (NCL) says, "These victims are not lonely, they're not out of touch with family and friends. They're just too polite to hang up — and they're handing the keys to the house to the burglar."

CELLULAR TELEPHONE STINGS:

Always do business with a company that is well known or that you are familiar with. There are many companies that illegally clone cellular telephones. (Set their cellular phone with your number for billing.) Be sure to deal with someone reputable and, if necessary, research any you do not know.

◆ Indications that someone may have cloned your cellular number:
- Frequent incoming calls are hanging up.
- Monitor your monthly phone bill for unmade calls.
- Difficulty in receiving voice mail.

◆ Do:
- Protect your personal identification number.
- Remove any outward evidence of a cellular phone when parking your car.
- Allow only your cellular technician to install or test the phone.
- Ask the service carrier to remove unwanted features such as international calls, call forwarding and three-way calling, etc.

AUTO REPAIR:

Automobile repair work and emergency road repair leads the lists of consumer complaints across this country. Women, especially, should be alert and aware of anyone who looks under the hood or who checks the tires. If you are in a strange garage, watch the person working and know what they are doing. They have been known to puncture a tire deliberately, pull wires from vital areas, etc. Stay up to date with regular maintenance using someone you know and trust.

For any repair, get an estimate in writing before work begins. Make it known immediately that any repairs beyond the estimate need your prior approval. Ask for the old parts or at least insist on inspecting them. Repair shops that are legitimate are more than eager to do this. Many shops are not registered or licenced. (Some states require registration.)

Ask a lot of questions. How will you determine what is wrong? What guarantee do you give on repairs? Does this need to be done right away? Is there another way to make the repair?

> **HINT:** *Get a second opinion for any major repair and/or automobile body damage.*

CREDIT CARDS:

How many credit cards do you have? Do you carry all of them with you? Cash is beginning to be something we used in the past as more and more of us depend on the credit cards or debit bank cards to do our shopping. Watch out for credit card offers in the mail. (See Chapter 10 "Credit Card and Credit Rating")

TRAVELERS:

There are con artists who travel north in the summer months and south in the winter months. They are almost like bands of gypsies. The groups and their businesses go on from one generation to the next. You can see them traveling together on the highway at times in their sleek new mobile homes and new trucks.

Example:
One of the biggest scams is the resealing of driveways. They stop at your home and tell you they are doing several driveways in the area and they can give you a good price if you act right away. They ask for a deposit and the balance to be paid upon completion. One of them will start working on the driveway while the other goes to the bank and cashes the check. When they are

> done, the driveway looks beautiful. You look at it and it seems like a good job, so you pay them the difference. They immediately cash your check and are gone. The first good rainfall washes all the paint away. All they did was paint the drive with a plain old motor oil and cheap paint.

Remember, these people want their money up front. They prefer cash. They work in small groups in a neighborhood looking for victims and then move on. Mobility is the key to their success because they can't operate in any one area long before law enforcement officials find them and lock them up. They know that.

HOME REPAIRS:

Homeowners are always ready to spruce up their homes or have repairs done economically. This opens them up and makes them more vulnerable to scams. Watch for the irresistible bargain. These people want their money up front or at least a large down payment. Then they disappear.

Check your Better Business Bureau to see if there have been any complaints. But, remember, the Bureau only lists the complaints they receive. If a person is new to town, changed the business name or received no complaints, doesn't make them a good business to deal with.

Beware of any contractor who just shows up at your door, will not leave his phone number or give you a business card. Beware of the person that comes to your door or calls and says, "We are doing the home down the street and while in the neighborhood he can give you a free estimate on your roof, lawn, etc. He can give you a good price while his equipment is close." He in-

sists you must make up your mind now if you want this good price. Authorities warn people to be alert to some of the following scams:
- ◆ Any quality-control inspection.
- ◆ Anyone telling you the roof trusses are sagging.
- ◆ Anyone telling you the roof is rotted and needs replacement.
- ◆ Insect or animal infestation.
- ◆ Rebate if you do the work now.
- ◆ A "bond" guaranteeing work that is not necessary and often not done.
- ◆ Additional flooring supports needed.

The home repair scam will give you a roof safety check free. They tell you they are able to detect any serious problems before they give you trouble or do damage. You let them do the safety check and they uncovered what they consider a serious problem. He assures you he can repair it quickly before it gets any worse and, luckily he's between jobs. All you need to do is sign an agreement. (by signing you will be obligated to pay thousands of dollars for roof repair. They can get a lien on your home or give a lender a second mortgage usually with an outrageous rate of interest.) (See Chapter 12 "Contracts")

Their favorite people are single women, the elderly and working couples too busy to check into credentials. You may not even realize you have been bamboozled until after a couple of good rain storms. Be sure to:
- ◆ Choose a contractor carefully by checking references, their licence, asking questions.
- ◆ Never sign for repairs without a second estimate.
- ◆ Never sign the same day you get an estimate or

during the first contact. Beware of any offer only good for the day.
- ◆ Check with the Better Business Bureau for any complaints.
- ◆ Get a written estimate which includes a time limit for completion.
- ◆ Make sure you have a written contract (i.e. date, names, price, material specifications to be used, exactly what will be done, building permit application, full material and labor costs, completion date, how payment will be made).
- ◆ Don't make a final payment until all the finishing touches are complete and the local permit office has inspected the job.
- ◆ Make sure you get a complete release saying the contractor has paid for all materials and/or subcontractors before you make a final payment. Ask for a contractor's affidavit before making a final payment.
- ◆ Proceed cautiously if the contractor arranges the financing.
- ◆ Don't be rushed into anything.

> **HINT:** *Do your research and don't sign a contract with the one that offers the lowest price just because the price is lower.*

PRIZES:

Wonderful news! The man on the phone sounded excited. He introduced himself and his company and then said, "You have just won a $50,000 prize. I have in my hand a cashier's check for $50,000. All you have to do is send a check for $4000 to cover the Federal income taxes and I can mail the check to you immediately." If it's too good to be true, be wary. This is too good. The $4,000 check was sent and cashed. The $50,000 was never received. This is part of a $40 million a year telemarketing plan under investigation by the FBI.

> **HINT:** *Never pay money to get a prize. You pay the money and you will never see the prize.*

LEGAL SERVICES:
Attorney Leigh P. Perkins wrote, *"The middle-class client has always been the hardest to land, and a growing number of lawyers are using a controversial alternative to set the initial hook."* Lawyers Weekly USA Section B, "In Practice," December 18,1995.

A new trend in legal services called "Unbundling" or "Discrete Task" is taking place across the country starting on the west coast. Consumers are staying away from traditional legal services and choosing to represent themselves. These people are ready and willing to forgo hiring attorneys. This revolution for an alternate way to resolve legal problems has the lawyers fearful and the whole legal system in an upheaval. Consequently, the beginning of "unbundling."

What is "unbundling" or "task sharing"? Lawyers have begun to offer and advertise that for a modest fee they are available to provide initial counseling advice and limited representation to self-represented people. "Unbundling" and "task sharing" services assist clients only when and where skilled help is needed. Attorneys provide court standardized forms to clients as well as instructional materials on filling out the forms, while others provide model pleadings and legal advice.

Is "unbundling" a new approach to serving the community or is it just a new "bait and switch" scam?

Law firms advertise their service. When a person goes in wanting only one service such as a form filled out, or a letter written to a landlord, the attorney tries to sell the person legal advice. He then offers alternative ways to handle the situation. You have taken the bait expecting to pay for the one service and end up paying for several services. And because you are representing yourself, you must sign a disclosure that the attorney is not the attorney of record and has no legal responsibility.

Small law firms are flocking to set up "unbundling" services to cater to Americans that would normally stay away from attorneys. *"If you're in Middle America, you can make money doing this,"* says Attorney Don Wyatt of Wolfeboro, New Hamshire. Lawyers Weekly USA Section B, "In Practice," December 18, 1995.

> **HINT:** *Make sure you have in writing what the lawyer will do and what you are to do. Know what you are paying for and how much it will cost you.*

FUND RAISERS-CHARITIES:

It is perfectly legal for a telemarketer to collect for a local charity. Remember, not all the money you give will go to the charity. Ask questions about how much goes to the fund-raiser or if they are collecting a fixed fee before giving your money. If you do give money, you will probably be put on a list for other fund-raising scams. **You can bypass** the telemarketer and send your check directly to the charity.

Telemarketers are required to disclose that they are paid solicitors, their name, the name of the telemarketing company and the organization for which they are soliciting. If the call says, "I'm calling for . . ." then they are a paid solicitor. When the caller says, "I'm from the . . ." they are part of an organization and you are speaking directly with the charity.

Urgent requests for donations to save our Social Security trust fund, save Medicare and prevent other imminent national disasters are flooding the mail service. They suggest you donate anywhere from $25 to $500 to help. Fund raiser's names and cries for help are in big bold type with the pitch usually signed by the chairman or president. Return envelope only shows a post office box. If the organization is not willing to give you the address of their headquarters, there might not be any. Be observant, be careful, and report any you feel are fraudulent operations. Social Security and Medicare are funded through work and administered by the government. They do not solicit additional funds. **Beware!**

> **HINT:** *Check the charity to make sure it is the one you really think it is and not someone posing as the charity or organization.*

Guidelines for both mail and phone solicitations:
- ◆ Beware of any charity that refuses to give you a breakdown of where the money goes. Use the rule of thumb that 60% of the money taken in is used in the programs.
- ◆ Do not relent and give in to pressure during telephone or personal solicitations that insist you send money immediately.

- Avoid donating to charities you don't know.
- Ask for the charities Federal tax identification number.
- If they say they will send a carrier to pick up the money. Refuse this offer.
- Ask and get a clear answer on tax deductibility. If you are in doubt, ask.
- Get the exact name of the organization.
- Know the purpose of the organization.
- Find out how it attempts to achieve that purpose.
- How much of your donation will be used for charitable purposes and how much is used for administration and fund-raising.
- High pressure techniques should alert you to a possible scam.
- Don't give a credit card or bank account number to anyone you don't know.
- Don't give cash.
- Don't be fooled by an organization name. The name can sound like a legitimate organization.
- Keep records of all donations and canceled checks or receipts.
- Call your state officials if you suspect a scam or if you are intimidated or pressured.
- Beware of requests to send money or buy something sight unseen unless you initiated the call.

WORK-AT-HOME SCAMS:

Large advertisements offer outrageous sums to stuff envelopes, address cards, assemble jewelry, etc. The company requires you to buy the necessary materials and to sign a contract. The small print in the contract gives the company the right to not accept your work because it doesn't meet their standard or it is the wrong number of items or for some other reason. These companies make their money from the sale of the materials. They don't intend to pay for your work.

The Federal Trade Commission especially warns against envelope-stuffing schemes. The FTC pamphlet, "Work-at-home-schemes," suggests you ask a potential employer the following information to help determine whether he or she is offering legitimate employment:

- ◆ What tasks will you be required to perform? (Ask for a complete list step by step.)
- ◆ Will you be working for salary or commission?
- ◆ Who will pay you?
- ◆ When will you be payed?
- ◆ What supplies and equipment will you have to purchase and what fees will you have to pay before earning any money?

Check all references, Ask for the names of some of the people that work for them. Contact the people personally and ask questions. It's your money and you can not afford to lose. It makes no sense for anyone to pay a large price to stuff or address envelopes. Never send money to a post office box.

JOB-OFFERS:

Never answer an ad with a 900 number. The ad may offer a good salary, but the long and rambling message will cost you, $20 to $50 on your next phone bill.

They will tell you an advanced fee must be paid for a guaranteed job. The money is gone and you are still out of a job. A legitimate broker will take a percentage out of your first few months pay or he will be paid by your new employer.

PREPAYMENT FUNERAL PLANS:

There are a number of state laws on how the funeral industry can handle and invest your funds. Like any other business, there are people out there who thrive on bogus plans. Be a wise consumer and check into their credentials before purchasing. Ask where the money is kept and what guarantees you have that the money and services will be available when you need them.

Even with these controls, mortuaries go out of business. You might move and funds might be non-returnable or your plan may not cover the inflated costs of the future. This could leave your survivors caught in a plan and having to foot the balance of the bill.

If you feel you want to set aside money for your final arrangements, you might want to set up a "Totten Trust." This can be set up in a trust or savings plan and earmarked for final arrangements. Most financial institutions will do this for a very small charge. These trust funds are easily transferred or withdrawn quickly when needed and you will have complete control over the money during your lifetime.

SWEEPSTAKES:

You receive a check in the mail. Actually it is a piece of paper designed to look like a check. It tells you to call the enclosed 900 number and they will send a real check right away. Later, your phone bill will show you paid for the call. You will probably get a check for a dollar and maybe some coupons but the call could cost as much as $25. Your name will then be sold by them to direct marketing lists. Only answer by mail and then it only costs the price of a stamp. The other alternative is to ignore the letter and throw it in the waste basket.

SCAMS

THE DEAD MAN'S PACKAGE SCAM:

This is one of the most common of all scams for the new widow or widower. There are even some scam-artists that work this on other new survivors. It goes like this: The scam-artist, a nicely dressed and somber individual turns up on your doorstep and tell you he is delivering a package. It was ordered just before the person's death. It was to be paid upon delivery. The family is usually too upset to ask questions and the scam-artist walks away with the cash or a check. The box when opened holds a bible, shredded papers or even a brick. One way to protect yourself is to open the package while the delivery agent is still there.

FINAL HINTS AND WHAT TO WATCH FOR:
- A money-back guarantee doesn't mean anything if you can't find the company.
- A con artist is polite, neat looking, soft-spoken, pretends to be a policeman, a bank manager, a phone company representative, a repairman and so forth.
- A fancy office or grimy basement makes no difference.
- Don't be afraid to say "NO!" Never worry about being embarrassed.
- If you fall for one scam you will probably be put on a list for others.
- If you are approached for money — leave your money in the bank and call police immediately.
- Legitimate repair men don't go door to door. If you need repair work, call a contractor and get an estimate. (See repairs)
- Always ask to see their a policeman's badge and

their picture ID. Call the telephone number in the phone book, not the one given to you.
◆ The most common scams are "the pidgin drop," "the bank examiner," and "the home improvement and repair scam."

**It's too good to be true,
then be wary because it usually isn't.**

For more information on scams, call or write to these agencies.
◆ National Consumer League's National Fraud Information Center 800-876-7060 (general information)
◆ Avoid frauds-publication-send $1 to *"Avoid Fraud"*, Pueblo, CO 81009
◆ The National Charities Information Bureau offers a *Wise Giving Guide.* Send a stamp addressed business envelope to NCIB, Dept.511, 19 Union Square West, New York, NY 10003.
◆ *Consumer Affairs Fact Sheet-Consumer Fraud: Telemarketing* (D15385) Write to AARP Fulfillment, 601 E. St. N.W., Washington, D.C. 20049.

CHAPTER 21

✳

TAXES

TAXES

Federal and state taxes are a necessary evil in all our lives. The more you know about the tax laws and how they apply, the better off you will be. Each person is responsible for any tax form they sign whether or not they prepare the form.

If you have not taken the time to go over each and every tax form prepared for you, now is the time to start. The IRS has three years from the day the tax return is due or the date of filing whichever is later to take action. If you sign a joint return and they can't get the money from your spouse, they will come after you. This includes any added taxes assessed because of an audit plus interest and penalties from the time of the original due date of the tax. Be careful!

The IRS never forgets, so it is vital that you never discard records to substantiate your deductions. Any time you depreciate an asset, you must keep all the information as long as you still have that asset plus all time limits for an audit. The same is true if you have postponed tax on anything such as your home or exchange of property. Records must be kept while they are active, and for at least three years thereafter. Important records to keep:

- ◆ Investment and mutual fund purchases or sales along with the record of the amount reinvested or

added, real property purchase and closing statements, all forms dealing with basis, capital improvements of property, sale of any major asset, postponement of taxes, depreciation claimed, casualty loses claimed, itemized deductions, etc.
- ◆ Supporting records for any tax form that is eligible for auditing. (Usually three years after filing, payment, or auditing, whichever is later.) Birth certificates, Social Security cards, marriage licenses, divorce papers, insurance policies, deeds, mortgages, appraisals, stock or bond certificates, legal correspondence or judgments, retirement and pension records, statements of retirement funds, wills and trusts.
- ◆ State income tax laws have different time limits. Check your local state for these.
- ◆ Unreported income of more than 25 percent of the income shown on your returns has a six-year limitation.
- ◆ Income tax fraud has no time limits.
- ◆ If you decide to clean out older than five year tax forms, keep, at least, the first two pages of all returns as well as any schedule dealing with depreciation, postponement or deferral of taxes.

WHO MUST FILE A RETURN?
- ◆ Individuals — Check for the requirements for your filing status, gross income and age.
- ◆ Surviving Spouses, Executors, Administrators, Legal Representatives — If you fall into one of these categories, you must file a final return for the deceased if the decedent met the filing requirements at the date of death.

- Self-employed persons — You must file if your gross income is $400 or more.

CHOOSING A TAX PREPARER:
- Ask: What kinds of clients do you represent? A tax preparer who only does simple returns based on W-2 and 1099 forms might not be able to do investment income, business returns, sale of home, and other types of complicated returns.
- Ask: Do you do all of the work on my return personally or is it given to someone else to do? A single preparer is usually best to answer the questions and those of the IRS about your return.
- Ask: What is your education and what recent tax training have you had? You want someone that has been doing taxes for a period of time and is current on tax laws and forms.

> **HINT:** *Be aware that you and not your tax preparer is legally responsible for your tax return and its accuracy.*

WHEN DO I HAVE TO FILE?

It is important to always file your individual income returns on time. The Internal Revenue Service assesses interest and penalties against all late or non-filing of tax forms. There are penalties for not filing as well as penalties for not paying. At least you can avoid the non-filing penalties by filing on time even if you don't have the money to pay the tax.
- No extension requested, due April 15th of the year following the close of the tax year.
- Form 4868 extension, due August 15th.

◆ Form 2688, second extension, due October 15th.

ESTATE TAXES:

Estate taxes are the Federal government's tax on the fair market value of property passing from a person that died to the heirs and beneficiaries. (IRS Form #706) The law allows us to pass our assets to whomever we wish at our death. There is an estate tax that must be paid for the privilege. (See IRS Publication 448, Federal Estate and Gift Taxes)

When an estate is opened, the first action a Personal Representative must do is to apply to the IRS for an identification number. This is done by filing an SS-4 form, *Application for Employer Identification Number*. The form is available through IRS or Social Security,

The total or what is known as the "gross estate" is made up of all the property of the deceased including, but not limited to, real estate, personal items, furnishings, stocks, bonds, jewelry, royalties and revocable trusts. Life insurance going to the estate, rather than an individual beneficiary, is also included.

Estate taxes are calculated on the "taxable estate." To get this figure, you must take the gross estate amount minus all deductions allowed and minus exclusions. Check with the IRS and your local state department of revenue for information on estates. The current rate is 18% on taxable estates of less than $10,000 and then 55% of taxable estates of more than $3,000,000 with a graduated scale for the amounts between. Tax rates on the taxable estate are high. Because of this, you will want to take full benefit of any exclusion available:

◆ Marital deduction — There is an unlimited marital deduction for property passing to the spouse.

If you have assets of more than $600,000, (graduating up to $1 million in the next 10 years) it is important for you to take this deduction into consideration in your estate planning. It is necessary to note that while there are no taxes due on the amount inherited by a spouse, when your spouse dies the amount will be added to the spouse's assets. In many cases all this will do is defer the taxes until the spouse dies. If that is the case, then more taxes may be due at a later date. Check with a financial or estate planner for assistance.

> **HINT:** *Remember, property tends to appreciate over time and the taxes could be on a higher amount.*

The basis of an asset (this is the amount you paid plus all capital improvements) after a death changes to an adjusted basis. This adjusted basis is then used when you sell the asset. At death it is transferred with a basis of the fair market value. As an example:

Jane and Bill owned a large home they originally purchased for $100,000. The title was held as husband and wife by the entireties. This means that after Jane died, Bill became the sole owner. The home was valued at $150,000 on the date of Jane's death. One half of the home has the basis of $50,000 while the other half that was Bill's now has a basis of $75,000. The new basis Bill will use when he sells the home is $125,000 instead of the original $100,000. ($50,000 + $75,000 = $125,000.)

◆ Charitable deduction — There is no limit to the amount of the deduction. You can give it to the charity outright or through a charitable remain-

der trust. Just as in the marital deduction, you can transfer assets to a charity through your will or a revocable trust. Use this deduction to your benefit. It is possible to set up a charitable trust with you as trustee with these benefits:
1. Current charitable contribution deduction (fair market value).
2. Lifetime income from the assets of the trust.
3. No estate tax on the trust assets.
4. No capital gains tax on the sale of trust assets.

You can transfer the assets to the charitable trust and take the deduction. The trust then sells the assets, usually without a tax consequence, and reinvests the money into income producing assets. Payments by the charity can then be made to you from the income based on a prearranged formula in the trust agreement.

Check with your charity, mutual fund broker or attorney to set up the trust.

◆ Unified credit — There is a $600,000 (graduating up to $1 million in the next 10 years) sheltered amount from the gross estate. It is called the "unified credit" because it encompasses both the gifts made during your lifetime as well as the property passed at your death.

◆ Gifts given by you are limited to $10,000 (cash or cash equivalent), per person, per year. Any amount over that requires a gift tax form sent to the IRS. While a form has to be filled out and filed with the IRS, there is no tax due. This amount over the $10,000 listed on these is kept in abeyance and will be subtracted from the $600,000 (graduating up to $1 million in the next 10 years) you are allowed at death or by gift. Tax planning can allow you to give an amount tax free, thereby eliminating the estate tax.

HOME:

Pre- May 6, 1997, sales: The IRS has special tax breaks dealing with the sale of your home. For these laws to be applicable the home must be your principal residence. Any type of principal residence can qualify. In addition to a single family dwelling, your home can be a mobile home, a condominium or cooperative or even a houseboat. Whether you postpone the tax or pay, you must complete and file IRS form 2119 the year after you sell the home. This is filed with your regular IRS filing. The land beneath your home need not be owned.

You may postpone any capital gain if you purchase a new principle residence within 24 months before or after the sale. There are no time extensions. The purchase price of the new home must be equal to or more than the proceeds from the old home. The mortgages are irrelevant when doing the calculations. However if the new home is less expensive than the old one, you will owe tax on your profit up to the difference in price.

Example:

Suppose you sell your home for $125,000 net with a profit after all expenses of $30,000. You buy a condominium for $130,000. The profit will then be postponed and the new home will have an adjusted basis. But, if you buy that condominium for $110,000, you will pay taxes on $15,000 of the profit and the other $15,000 will be postponed to the new home. ($125,000 net minus the $110,000 new home.)

For taxpayers over the age of 55 there is a one time writeoff of up to $125,000 in home sale profit. If either you or your spouse, while married, has taken this exclusion, then you can not take it again. (Get IRS Publication 523, Sale of Home.)

Starting May 6, 1997 sales: The tax rules for the selling ones home changed on May 6, 1997. The rule allows homeowners to avoid taxes on home sale profits up to $500,000 for married couples filing jointly and $250,000 for individuals. In order to qualify, you must have lived in the home for two of the last five years.

This rule repeals a provision that has been in effect for many years. You will no longer be allowed to postpone any gain by rolling it into a new home. All sales will be accounted for completely in the year of sale.

RETIREMENT FUNDS:

When retirement funds are withdrawn, they are taxable and added to your income. If it comes from an employer's plan or if it is drawn in a lump-sum, it can be averaged at a five or seven-year tax rate. (See IRS Publication 575)

The general rule is that any retirement fund withdrawn prior to age 59½ incurs a 10% penalty. If you find you must draw this money early to live on, check with the IRS. Other options are available.

Inherited IRAs have their own IRS rules. A spouse has the option of rolling the IRA into his/her own IRA. This subjects it to the same rules as if it had been deposited as a regular IRA. If an inherited IRA is cashed instead of being rolled over, it must be added to the spouse's income. If an IRA is inherited by someone other than a spouse, it cannot be rolled over. It must be withdrawn within a certain period and taxes paid. (See IRS Publication 590)

IRA transfers, resulting from a divorce settlement, can be rolled into a receiving spouse's plan without a penalty.

BANKRUPTCY:

An individual who files bankruptcy under Chapter 7 or 11 of the Bankruptcy Code creates a separate "estate" consisting of property that belonged to him prior to the bankruptcy filing date. The bankruptcy estate is now a new taxable entity. The estate may produce its own income as well as incur its own expenses. This gives the individual a fresh start, with certain exceptions — wages he earns and property he acquires after the bankruptcy case has begun. (See IRS Publication 908)

CHAPTER 22

∗

BANKRUPTCY

BANKRUPTCY

The last few years have lessened the personal stigma associated with filing bankruptcy. Federal laws allows a person or couple to wipe out most of their debts and make a new start. Bankruptcy is filed in a Federal court which has the ultimate jurisdiction to forgive debts and make a distribution of the debtor's property. Federal bankruptcy laws provide a legal procedure by which a debtor obtains relief from the demands of creditors.

During the process of trying to pay bills that have gotten too large, you may decide, "I will file bankruptcy and then I can start all over again." Maybe so, but, if that happens, it can ruin your chances to buy a home, a car, or even get a credit card. You should consider bankruptcy only as a last resort. It can stay with your credit history for up to 10 years. Before leaping into a bankruptcy situation, look into any available alternatives.

ALTERNATIVES:
- ◆ Check with the creditor and try to renegotiate payments and/or interest on the account.
- ◆ Contact the Consumer Credit Counseling Service. This is a nationwide nonprofit organization listed in the local telephone directory.
- ◆ Contact your attorney to see if there are any other options in your state.

> **HINT:** *Personal bankruptcy may be filed by either or by both of you.*

If you file for bankruptcy, the advantages include your ability to start all over again. Most of your debts will be forgiven. The Federal laws exempt some of your property, such as your home, car, furnishings, and the tools you use in your trade or business from your creditors. Each state has some variation on these exemptions and you must be sure to check them out with your attorney or in your local law library.

Bankruptcy can wipe out credit card bills, attorney bills, doctor bills, student loans, etc. It *cannot* wipe out any property that has a secured lien, such as a mortgage, a car loan, etc. Bankruptcy cannot wipe out local, state, or Federal tax bills or liens. The Bankruptcy Court has the authority to dispose of your personal assets.

If bankruptcy has been filed by an ex-spouse, who has been ordered to pay child support or alimony, you can fight back. Pursuant to the Bankruptcy Law 11 USC §362 (b)(2), the automatic stay provisions do not apply to the collection of alimony, maintenance, or support from property that is not property of the bankrupt's estate. This means that you can collect alimony, maintenance, or support from the salary of a debtor.

Lump-sum alimony is usually a distribution of assets of the marriage. Charles Tatlebaum, vice president of the American Bankruptcy Institute said, "Alimony and child support may not be discharged by bankruptcy, but property settlements may be forgiven. As a result, "some lawyers are playing games."

Your spouse may wipe his name off the credit cards

but, that does not take your name from them. The companies will come after you for collection if your name is on them or if you have ever used them.

BAD REASONS FOR FILING BANKRUPTCY:
- Debts are primarily from unpaid taxes, alimony or child support.
- If you want to eliminate a debt such as your mortgage, you are usually required to allow the creditor to take possession of the property and sell it. It would be better for you to go the lender and try to renegotiate your payments or, maybe, you could sell the property yourself before it is repossessed.
- If you want to avoid collection agency harassment there are better methods. The Federal law prohibits bill collectors from harassing you by telephone or approaching you in person.
- If you want to avoid a large debt you recently incurred this route may not work. Bankruptcy courts do not allow you to avoid paying debts you ran up in anticipation of filing for bankruptcy.
- If you want to avoid garnishment or a wage assignment, remember, only 25% of your wages can be used to satisfy a court judgment, except for alimony and child support.

NON-DISCHARGEABLE DEBTS:
- Federal, state and local taxes.
- Student loans made or insured by the government.
- Debts denied or waived in a previous bankruptcy.
- Alimony or child support.
- Debts from willful and malicious injury, drunken driving, larceny or embezzlement.

STEPS TO AVOID BANKRUPTCY:
- ◆ Work out a realistic budget. Include an amount for emergencies. Then stick to it.
- ◆ Keep your personal debt limit at no more than 20% of your take-home pay.
- ◆ Keep your mortgage no more than a third of your take-home pay.
- ◆ When you need to borrow, shop around for the best interest and terms available.
- ◆ Start a savings account and pay this account each month.

> **HINT:** *Not only creditors, but potential employers and customers avoid persons who have filed bankruptcy.*

Suddenly Alone

CHAPTER 23

※

PRENUPTIAL AGREEMENTS

PRENUPTIAL AGREEMENTS

So you plan to be married soon. Think carefully about entering into a prenuptial agreement. How do you protect the assets you have worked so hard for all these years? Maybe this is your first marriage or second or more. No matter which marriage it is, take time to talk about your needs and desires for the future. Courts will uphold a prenuptial contract. It is up to the two of you to sit down to discuss present and future finances and how you want them handled.

A prenuptial agreement is a formal contract signed by both of you and witnessed stating how each person's assets and debts will be handled and dispersed if death, separation, or divorce happens. It can also deal with the co-mingled marital property and how this can be dispersed and to whom. In other words, it is a binding contract on how your finances will be taken care of if something happens to separate the two of you. (See Chapter 12 "Contracts")

Prenuptials have been around almost since the beginning of time. Marriages were arranged for economic, social and survival reasons. Marriage contracts were made between the parties involved or the parents. Now, marriage starts as more "romantic love" rather than economic. Even though we believe in romance, marriage is still an economic partnership and the finances

Prenuptial Agreements

need to be protected. Marriage is only partly about love and togetherness. It is about a money partnership. It is also about working together to accomplish goals and accumulating material property

> **HINT:** *Be careful and prepare a prenuptial properly to avoid the document being challenged later in court.*

This chapter is dedicated to the single person who has been in the work force or the person who is about to marry again. Think about what you have acquired over the years and how you plan to protect it. If you have children prior to this marriage, make your plans known now on how you want these assets protected and who they will eventually go to.

Widows and widowers often rush into another marriage out of loneliness and desperation without thinking about the financial ramifications. Personal assets quickly get changed into joint ownership. Mixing love and money doesn't always work. A second marriage demands a practical, business approach to finances. Take time to think about this mixture and work out the details for the best interests of both of you. Remember, sometimes romance can be risky, so go slowly.

In later life, the prenuptial agreement is imperative. It is not a plan for divorce. It is a plan for the future finances of the marriage. It is protection for each of you to cover the assets built over past years. It allows you to protect your assets for your children. You can cover the appreciation of separate assets, if you become disabled, how bills will be paid, education for the children and any other lawful provision you both agree on.

More and more people are taking that trip down the isle into marriage. Many of these couples are entering into a prenuptial agreement. It is not only the rich and famous that have assets and families to protect. You must realize that as time goes by, circumstances and feelings may change. Sickness, death, and divorce do happen.

These agreements can be amended and changed to fit the circumstances. Protecting the assets you have worked hard for is not wrong. The prenuptial agreement is written before marriage when both parties are loving, trusting and rational. You are better able to discuss the financial possibilities that might occur. Without a prenuptial agreement you are bound by the property laws of your state if something happens.

Each state has laws on the distribution of property rights of a spouse and children after the death of one of the parties. Even a will can be broken if it does not agree with the laws. A contract between the two of you, which is reasonable, will hold up in court.

The courts usually divide all marital property 50/50 in a divorce, even if only one of the spouses earned all the money. A prenuptial agreement allows you to adjust these percentages as long as it is reasonable.

Start early to communicate the idea of an agreement. It is not a subject you want to talk about the day or so before the wedding. Discuss the subject when you are not emotional or distraught. Insist on full disclosure of assets, debts and income. Review of each other's tax returns provides not only information, but a feeling of trust. Talk to your own lawyer — his job is to protect you. A small amount of advance planning can make the future more secure and the relationship firmer.

Prenuptial Agreements

> **HINT:** *Talk before the marriage about finances and plans for future disposal of your assets and debts.*

The famous divorce attorney, Reoul Felder, answered the question of whether he would recommend prenuptial agreements when he said, "Given today's divorce rate, anybody who goes into a marriage without a prenuptial agreement is doing something very foolhardy. Back before these modern laws of equitable distribution, it was very simple. Women got support until remarriage or death. Now both men and women can get support or alimony. It can be for rehabilitation or permanent. Even then they may never collect it."

Agreements on how to deal with money during your future marriage is essential. Making up an agreement ahead of time allows you to think about financial goals, how children will be cared for, future investment goals and how any appreciation of separate property will be handled. It also allows you to think about future support for one of you if needed.

A prenuptial agreement is a blueprint for the distribution of the assets owned by both parties, both before and after marriage. Judges, lawyers, and financial planners agree that most couples who marry for the second time should have something in writing. See the sample form at the end of the chapter.

> **HINT:** *Love can be better the second time around. With a prenuptial agreement, it may be even better. Agreements have validity in almost all states, if they are properly drafted.*

EFFECTIVE AND USEFUL PRENUPTIAL AGREEMENTS:
- ◆ Include a full and accurate disclosure of the value of assets and the extent of debts by each of you. Work toward a voluntary and independent evaluation and representation of your assets. Include the disposition of all the assets and liabilities in the event of death, divorce or separation. Check into and include all possibilities, such as these:
    1. Real property including the home.
    2. Business ownership.
    3. Fair market value of investments.
    4. Antiques or collections.
    5. Premarital property.
    6. Personal property.
- ◆ Each party should have the benefit of a truly independent attorney.
- ◆ List all real property and whose name is on the titles and who would receive the property in the event of death, divorce or separation.
- ◆ Include income received and disposition of the income during the marriage.
- ◆ Designate the rights and responsibilities of each party.
- ◆ List life insurance and the owners of policies as well as the current beneficiaries. If you plan on protecting either of you with additional life insurance, put this into the agreement as well as who will be the owner and/or beneficiaries of each policy.
- ◆ Account for the rights at death for children of a previous marriage. This should be done in conjunction with a will or trust to protect all con-

PRENUPTIAL AGREEMENTS

cerned. (See Chapter 13, "Estate Planning")
◆ In order to avoid disputes in the event of divorce or the illness of one of the spouses, cover these subjects in the agreement:
   1. The financial responsibilities for maintaining any property during the marriage as well as after if it comes to that.
   2. Control and management of any business or investment no matter whether it was jointly or separately acquired.
   3. Financial support of either party.
   4. Sale or purchases of both marital and separate property.
   5. Living arrangements and health care.
◆ Retirement benefits and retirement plans.
◆ Health insurance.
◆ Acknowledgment of any career arrangement. At least, get a verbal commitment to any arrangement made. Add to the agreement, the value of putting either the husband or wife through school.
◆ Agreement if pre-marriage property will ever become marital property.
◆ Agreement as to the increase of value of separate assets and how that increase will be treated if there is a separation or divorce.

> **HINT:** *You can update a prenuptial agreement by amending the document or with a postnuptial agreement.*

People don't want to deal with the issues that create the problems. It may not sound romantic or trusting, but these premarital documents can help the chances for a successful marriage because the discussion and agreement up front solves potential problems before they arise. Don't wait until you pick up the marriage license to sign a prenuptial agreement and then run down the aisle. Take time to put your desires into the contract. Avoid any possible duress in your decisions.

Churches, synagogues, schools, etc. offer premarital instruction prior to marriage. This chapter is also an instruction for pre-marriage. It teaches you communication as you discuss finances. It allows you to build a marriage partnership and a stronger relationship. It helps you know how each of you feel about money and your future needs, wants and goals.

There is no right or wrong in an agreement. It is only what the two of you want. Both of you should be represented by separate attorneys. One attorney can do it all, but each of you should have your rights protected by a separate attorney if there is any question or doubt. The prenuptial agreement is a delicate affair and it is very difficult to break in the future. A properly drafted and fair agreement can cut down on part of the inevitable hassle. This is a binding contract, unless there is fraud, misrepresentation, an irregularity or duress. It can be a contract even without counsel, so protect your rights ahead of time. Think and plan for the future.

Prenuptial Agreement
(Sample Form)

THIS PRENUPTIAL AGREEMENT is entered into on this the 28th day of October, 1998, by **JOHN Q. PUBLIC** of Minneapolis, Minnesota and **MARY B. GOOD** of Sarasota, Florida.

1. It is the intention of these parties to enter into a marriage contract. Each of the parties is fully advised of the assets owned by the other or as fully advised thereon as he or she desires and by his or her signature to this instrument, each conclusively agrees that he or she had any and all information relative to assets of the other as he or she desires to have disclosed to him or her prior to the marriage ceremony. Likewise, except as otherwise expressly provided herein, by his or her signature to this instrument, each conclusively waives any and all rights to any portions of the estate of the other at demise or before and conclusively waives any and all statutory rights that he or she may have in the estate of the other at demise, regardless of whether or not such statutory rights are attempted to be created or granted by existing laws or laws enacted in the future.

2. The consideration for this agreement shall be the mutual waivers and agreements of the parties. Subsequent to their marriage, each shall continue to own his or her own properties and assets regardless of the marital status and free from any claims or rights except as otherwise expressly provided

in this agreement. Each may and shall be entitled to convey or transfer any or all such assets without the approval or consent of the other.
3. The parties specifically, expressly and conclusively for all purposes agree that the home and furnishings of GOOD in Sarasota, Florida, as between them and their heirs or Personal Representatives, shall not be deemed homestead property which may be required by law to pass by statute rather than by Will of the owner. Said home and furnishings shall continue to be the individual property of GOOD and may be conveyed, transferred or willed by her free of any homestead claims of PUBLIC. If the Sarasota home of GOOD is still owned by her at her demise and PUBLIC shall survive her, she shall by will grant PUBLIC exclusive personal use of the premises for his lifetime but such right is personal, may not be transferred or assigned and shall be waived if not personally used as a principal place of residence. If PUBLIC remains in the home after GOOD'S demise, he will be responsible for all mortgages, taxes, insurance and maintenance and if PUBLIC fails to do so his right to reside in the home shall be canceled. However, such promise to Will shall not impair or preclude GOOD'S right to convey or encumber the realty prior to her demise and shall not preclude her grant by Will of the fee simple title to others subject to that right of use.
4. PUBLIC owns a one/half undivided interest with his former wife in a residence in Sarasota County, Florida subject to the life estate of his mother. If he shall still own said interest at his death and GOOD

shall survive him as his widow, he shall grant his interest therein by Will to GOOD.

5. PUBLIC recognized that this marriage will terminate income of GOOD awarded to her by the Teachers Association from her prior Husband and agrees that upon a dissolution of the contemplated marriage of these parties or upon his demise with GOOD being his surviving widow, he and his decedent's estate shall pay GOOD a minimum of five hundred dollars ($500.00) per month for her lifetime or until her remarriage, whichever is earlier. If there shall be a dissolution of their marriage by court judgment PUBLIC conclusively agrees that a judgment shall be entered ordering him to pay GOOD a minimum of five hundred dollars ($500.00) per month for her lifetime or until she remarries, whichever is earlier, and the obligation shall continue after PUBLIC'S death and become an obligation of his estate.

6. This agreement is contingent upon these parties marrying each other withing 180 days after the execution of this agreement.

7. In the event of divorce of these parties from each other, neither shall be entitled to any benefits from the other by way of alimony or otherwise, except as herein expressly provided.

8. During their marriage each of the parties shall have full and free control and management of any and all of his or her assets of any and all kinds except as herein otherwise expressly provided.

9. The parties declare and hereby conclusively admit that they have read this agreement carefully, have fully disclosed the extent, nature and value

of all their properties, have discussed the legal effect of this agreement, are advised of their rights at demise under existing law to assets owned by the other and have executed this agreement upon their own free will and accord without any duress or persuasion.
10. This instrument is drafted by an attorney employed by GOOD. However, PUBLIC is fully advised that he should have independent counsel giving him legal advice but has seen fit to waive it, being confident that he is fully advised as to the assets and of his rights and obligations, not desiring any portion of the assets of GOOD either during marriage, upon divorce (if any) or upon his demise, other than as herein expressly provided, and confident that he does not need legal advice.

WHEREFORE, the parties have signed this agreement on this the 28th day of October, 1998.

Witnesses as to the signatures of both parties.

MARY B. GOOD

JOHN Q. PUBLIC

Attestation Clause

SIGNED, SEALED, PUBLISHED AND DECLARED by the above, MARY B. GOOD and JOHN Q. PUBLIC, as and for their Prenuptial Agreement, in the presence of each of us, who at their request and in their presence and in the presence of each other, have hereunto subscribed our names as attesting witnesses this the 28th day of October, 1998.

_____ Residing at Sarasota, Florida.

_____ Residing at Sarasota, Florida.

STATE OF FLORIDA
COUNTY OF SARASOTA

I HEREBY CERTIFY that on this day personally appeared before me, the undersigned authority, **JOHN Q. PUBLIC**, known by me to be the person described in or proven by _____ and who executed the foregoing instrument, and he duly acknowledged before me that he executed the same freely and voluntarily and for the purposes therein expressed.

WITNESS my hand and official seal in the County and State above set forth, on this the _____ day of _____, 1998.

My Commission Expires: Notary Public
State of Florida at Large

STATE OF FLORIDA
COUNTY OF SARASOTA

    I HEREBY CERTIFY that on this day personally appeared before me, the undersigned authority, **MARY B. GOOD**, known by me to be the person described in or proven by _____ and who executed the foregoing instrument, and she duly acknowledged before me that she executed the same freely and voluntarily and for the purposes therein expressed.

    WITNESS my hand and official seal in the County and State above set forth, on this the _____ day of _____, 1998.

_____

My Commission Expires: Notary Public
State of Florida at Large

CHAPTER 24

CO-HABITATION AGREEMENTS

CO-HABITATION AGREEMENTS

The fast-moving mobile society we are in has spanned a variety of significant other domestic relationships. No longer do two people need to have a marriage license to live together. In fact, by choice, many couples prefer the significant other relationship. People are sidestepping the marriage contract and instead deciding that living together works better for them. This can be a better arrangement for some couples. It is important to note that there are several items to consider before each party is protected. Unlike the institution of marriage there is no law to protect the cohabitation's interest. Their interests, financially and socially, are up to the two people involved. When the world is right and everything is going along smoothly, there is no problem, but when it starts going wrong, then one party is left out in the cold.

During many long term cohabitation relationships, the parties usually contribute to joint accounts, purchase property together, pay off obligations of each other and generally conduct themselves in a form of partnership arrangement. However, this is not a partnership as defined by law or by the Internal Revenue Rules.

In a marriage, there are laws to protect the spouse. In the case of death, the state has laws that cover the distribution of the deceased assets and the rights of the

Co-habitation Agreements

survivors. In a divorce, the law allows for distribution of marital assets and possible spousal support. When a relationship ends, there are no such protections.

In order to avoid unfortunate disputes if the relationship comes to an end or even if there is illness of one of the partners, it is vital to create a written agreement. (See form at the end of chapter) It is much easier to protect the rights of both of you at the beginning than after things have turned sour. This is especially true for people with special needs of health care expenses, business obligations, personal obligations or same-sex couples. Do an agreement that will cover the following:

- The financial responsibilities for maintaining the "community" home and estate.
- Clear delineation of rights and responsibilities of each party,
- Who is to manage and control business ventures or investments (jointly acquired or those brought into the relationship.)
- The acquisition of real property (such as a residence) as well as how it is to be titled and what will happen to it at death or ending of the relationship.
- Financial support if one of you becomes disabled or unemployed.
- Education, custody and support of any children of the relationship or from a prior relationship.
- Life insurance including who the owner and/or beneficiary of each policy.
- Health insurance and medical bills.
- Detail the terms in case the relationship ends by death or for any other reason.

No agreement will ever cover all of the issues that can possibly come up. Add the items that are important to the two of you. Take into account the needs and goals of each. Make sure it is something you both can live and comply with. Be sure to allow each partner enough time to evaluate the agreement, but be sure to set a time limit for signing.

> **HINT:** *Be clear and precise in the wording of the contract. Make sure it is fair and will hold up in the legal system.*

These agreements are contracts. (See Chapter 12, "Contracts") The validity of such an agreement will be decided on the facts of each case. It is best to hire separate attorneys so you will each be protected and the agreement will comply with state laws. Include terms that are enforceable and binding. The attorneys will serve as negotiators and counselors, not as hostile adversaries. If successful, the lawyers will craft an agreement which will promote financial security and your desire for a happy and enduring relationship. These agreements are commonly used now and can be used in conjunction with a Last Will and Testament or any other form of estate planning.

Case of a Significant Other Disaster

Alicia and Edward decided it would be best if they lived together instead of being legally married. Alicia had two grown children by a previous marriage. She had a job with the local hospital as an account receptionist making a small wage and was living in a rental apartment. Edward also had a grown

Co-habitation Agreements

son. Edward lived in his own home which was completely mortgage-free and they decided that Alicia would move in with him. He was employed as an accountant with a very good salary. They decided that each would put a percentage of their income into the pot to take care of the day to day living expenses. Any other expenses would be taken care of separately. If necessary, together they would make decisions for large expenditures.

They held themselves out as married and she even legally changed her last name to his. Years went by and each of them lived by the initial agreement, even though it was never put into writing. Neither one updated their wills to expressly put down what they wanted for protection of the other.

A few items were bought together, but if they were titled, only one name was put on the title. All other property was kept separate. The home continued to be only in Edward's name.

Then Edward died suddenly. Alicia was devastated. She was entitled to no benefits because she was not a legal spouse. They had always talked about her staying in the home and she counted on that. The will was probated, no provision was made for Alicia. She was not a widow, she was the significant other. His son inherited the house and he wanted it now. There was no way for her to prove their verbal agreement or if she owned any of the furnishings. She was out on the street and had to look for a place to live. Inflation had taken a toll and she found she could no longer afford a nice apartment. She had to face the fact that her life style changed and she had no protection under the law.

Co-habitation Agreement
(Make a copy.)

THIS AGREEMENT is made between <u>First party</u>, and <u>Second party</u>, on <u>Month</u>, <u>Day</u>, 199_, who reside in the city of_____, county of_____, state of___.

WHEREAS, the parties wish to live together, but so not wish to be bound by the statutory provisions of marriage, it is hereby agreed that the parties in the Agreement shall live together for an indefinite period of time subject to the following terms and conditions:

1. Property: All property listed on the attached as Exhibit "A" is incorporated in this Agreement by reference. The property on Exhibit "A" hereinafter belongs to the party under whose name it is listed prior to the making of the Agreement. All listed property is and shall continue to be the separate property of the person who owns it. All property received by either of us by gift or inheritance during our relationship shall be the separate property of the one who receives it. All real and/or personal property acquired by either of us during the relationship shall be considered to be our separate/joint property, except as follows:
    a)
    b)
2. Income: All income earned and accumulated during the existence of our relationship shall be maintained in one fund, and all debts and expenses arising during the existence of our union shall be paid from this fund. Each of us shall have an equal interest in this fund, and equal rights to its management and control, and each of us shall be equally entitled to any surplus that remains after the payment of all our debts and expenses.
3. Termination: Our relationship may be terminated at the sole will and decision of either of us, expressed by

a written notice given to the other with the following provisions for division of the assets of our relationship
   a)
   b)
4. Modification: This Agreement may be modified by an agreement in writing signed by both parties, with the exception that no modification may decrease the obligations that may be imposed regarding any children born of our union.
5. Application of Law: The validity of this Agreement shall be determined solely under the laws of the state of____. If any portion of this Agreement is held invalid or unenforceable in a court of law, then the rest of this Agreement shall remain in full force and effect to the extent practicable.
6. Claims: Neither party shall maintain any action or claim against the other for support, alimony, compensation, or for rights to any property existing prior to this date or acquired on or subsequent to the date of termination, except as stated in this Agreement.
7. Disclosure: The parties enter into this Agreement of their own free will and accord without reliance on any other inducement or promise, and with full disclosure of the interest each holds in any and all property, real, personal or mixed.
8. Right to Counsel: Each party to this Agreement has had the opportunity to have Independent Counsel review this Agreement.

Signed this ___ Day of ___ , 199___.

_____
First party

_____
Second party

CHAPTER

✷

CONCLUSION

CONCLUSIONS

I will end this book with a letter I received from my brother just before his death from prostate cancer. To be left is hard and while this was not a spouse or parent, I had lost my best friend. I had taken the opportunity to say goodbye to him in my own letter dealing with my feelings and our mutual dreams. Here is his reply exactly as he wrote the letter to me.

Dear Catherine,

Yes, it does seem that as we age we think more deeply of the fabric we have woven to make our life, and how both the good & bad talents of the weaver affect the cloth. There is no reason to feel badly about any of life's tragedies for life is just a series of tragedies interspersed with intervals of joy, happiness & high drama. For those of us who are so fortunate that we seem always able to remember life continues to be a blessing. A little pain & a little heartache are food for the soul. We all would like to have gone through life without erring — even once. Sad to say, though, we are only human. We have not been this way before. It's only trial & error with a few small successes thrown in that fills life's cup to the brim.

Do not ever believe that I have not had a full life. Do not think that I would have demanded more than I have freely been given by my family, my friends & even some I may not like too well.

CONCLUSION

Where else but on this earth could I have found the challenges, the peace & contentment, and the occasional heartbreak. Here is where we are and we will all founder through.

Your worries of having offended me in any way are not warranted. Yes, we are at times abrasive one to another. These times are inconsequential as compared to finished quilt. Be glad that we are all here. Be overjoyed that we can think well of each other. And one day when it is all over — as it surely will be — you will still be remembered by so many that you cannot count them all.

It takes a long time to put on paper the many thoughts that run through my mind. Your recent letter recalling events of our childhood remind me of pleasant times of the past. And it brings out the facts that in many ways we traveled different paths. Your experiences with Mom & Dad diverged from mine when I went to war. The results of that change in my life are apparent even today. My alliances changed as I took on new & exciting responsibilities. It did not mean that I had abandoned old alliances. It was just that the world whirls by. I remember often our early days and they were good days. I recall the few disappointments I had — they were insignificant compared to the marvelous opportunities that opened up to me at school — at Iowa — with Beth — with life as we lived it. I know of no other way to have lived it and still have extracted so much from the experience.

Your life, like mine, is covered with hills & valleys of success & failure. They can be seen in the assembly of your quilting, your books, your home & your friends. Do not ever despair that you have not given full measure to us all. If you feel that you should have done more it only means that that is the human condition. I too wish I had done more — been more available & understanding. Keep in mind how available you were and how much you are still offering to me &

my family — how much you offered to Frank & Ed & how much you would like to offer to Lucille.

Did it ever occur to you how self centered I have been and how over important I believed I was? As I look back I can see the many ways I could have been more helpful. Those days are past & I cannot change them. I can only do what I can do today and tomorrow. Whatever I do will never be enough to repay the indulgences heaped on me through my life. Be good to yourself. Do not heap blame when where the opposite is needed and deserved.

On this especially beautiful August day I would like you to be at peace with yourself and the world. Stardust has filtered down and agglomerated into the stuff of life. It surrounds me with the certain knowledge that all that we experienced or will yet experience is worth any suffering — any disappointment. Your world is really not a whole lot unlike mine. You have reached out to hold onto a big chunk of it. Hang on as best you can and enjoy it to the full.

There is an eternity out there for those who went before — and for us. We will all be replaced with those whose experiences will mirror ours. The continuance of all these life sustaining processes should gladden your heart as you press on through the journey.

We think of you often. We love you.

John

GLOSSARY

GLOSSARY

ACCELERATION CLAUSE: A clause in a contract that allows the lender to hasten or enforce early payment.

ACCEPTANCE: A legal term that says,"I will accept your offer."

ACTION: A legal preceding held to enforce or protect someone's right, to redress or prevent a wrong, to punish a crime.

ADJUSTED BASIS: The cost value of property plus all capital improvements minus all depreciation claimed on income tax forms.

ADMINISTRATION: The legal process of starting, maintaining and completing the probate process through the court.

ADMITTING THE WILL: A legal term describing the filing of a deceased person's will in the court system.

ADVERSARIES: The two parties on opposite sides of a law suit.

AFFIANT: A person who makes a statement under oath in an affidavit (document).

AFFIDAVIT: A sworn statement in writing under oath.

AGENT: A person who is authorized to act on behalf of another person or business.

ALIMONY/MAINTENANCE: Payments made by one spouse to another in discharge of the paying spouse's obligation under law to support the other spouse.

Glossary

AMEND: To alter or improve an existing document.

ANNUITY: A contract by which you pay an amount, either in one payment or over a period of years, to an insurance company. In return, the company agrees that on a specific date they will pay you a regular sum over a period of time.

ANTENUPTIAL AGREEMENT: Also known as a Prenuptial Agreement. An agreement entered into before the parties marry.

ARM: Adjustable Rate Mortgage

ARREARAGE: The amount of unpaid child support and/or alimony. Money past due on a debt.

ASSETS: Anything owned by the parties that has monetary value such as real, personal, or intangible property.

ATM: Automatic teller machine.

ATTESTATION: To affirm by witnessing that something in writing such as a signature or document is either authentic or true.

ATTORNEY/LAWYER: Person admitted by the state's highest court or by a Federal court to practice law in that jurisdiction.

BANKRUPTCY: A legal process under Federal law intended to insure fairness for creditors and to help the debtor by enabling him to start again with property he is allowed to retain by state law and exempt him from liabilities of preexisting debts. (Check your state laws).

BASIS: The cost value of property plus all capital improvements.

BENEFICIARY: A person or organization designated to receive property or money such as proceeds from an estate, trust, or insurance policy.

BEQUEST: A gift of money or other personal property (not real property) left to someone through a will.

CAPACITY: The qualifications such as age or competency, that are necessary for a person's actions to be legally permitted and recognized. Mental ability to make a rational decision, which includes the ability to perceive and appreciate all relevant facts.

CASH RESERVE: An amount of money set aside for emergencies.

CASH VALUE: A term used by insurance companies to describe the amount of cash available in a "whole life policy."

CD: Certificate of Deposit available through a financial institution bearing a set amount of interest.

CHILD SUPPORT: The obligation of both parents to support the children after a divorce. This term is usually used in reference to the payments from the non-residential parent to the primary residential parent.

CHURNING: Excessive trading in a stock or insurance account, by a broker, to generate commissions with relatively little concern for the welfare of his customer.

CLAIM: A report and form to apply for relief such as a debt owed by an estate or to compensate you from damage covered by insurance.

CLERK OF THE COURT: The office in your court house where legal papers and law suits are filed.

COHABITATION: Two persons living together outside the bounds of matrimony, A significant other relationship between two persons.

COHABITATION AGREEMENT: A written agreement about the terms and conditions of your cohabilitation and the distribution of property if the cohabilitation ends.

Glossary

CODICIL: A supplement to a will the purpose of which is to alter or change an already executed will.

COMPETENT MIND: Capacity to understand and to act reasonably. Capable of doing a certain thing.

COMPLAINT: Also known as a petition. The formal paper stating the initial legal action of the petitioner to the court that starts the legal divorce action or other law suit.

CONSIDERATION: A legal term referring to something of value that each person hopes to receive from a contract.

CONTRACT: A transaction involving two or more individuals whereby each becomes obligated to the other with reciprocal rights. The total legal obligation which results from the parties agreement as affected by law.

CONTRACTOR: One who is a party to a contract or makes an agreement with another to do a piece of work.

CONVERTIBLE CLAUSE: A term used in securities such as bonds or stocks that can be exchanged for another security in the same corporation. The ability to convert one type of insurance policy to a different type within the same company..

COSTS: Expenses accrued in litigation: filing, depositions, discovery, etc. Does not include the lawyer's fees.

COUNTER-PETITION: A counter claim made by a Respondent or Defendant on his behalf asking the court for relief.

CREDIT: Your ability to borrow money or make a purchase now and pay it back later.

CREDIT RATING: Information about your income, expenses and bill-paying history. Use of a point system to determine whether you have an ability or history to pay the money back.

CREDIT CARD: An open account loan that allows you to charge and pay at the billing period or over time with interest added.

CREDITORS: An individual or business with a legal right for payment of services, sales or loans.

CURTSEY: The right by which a man is entitled to a share in his wife's property after her death. (See Dower)

DEATH CERTIFICATE: The document by a physician as to the time, date and cause of death.

DEBTS: Money or property owed to a lender or for services and material purchased.

DECLARANT: A person who makes a declaration, particularly someone who makes a living will.

DEED: A written document that transfers title (ownership) of real estate property.

DEFERRED COMPENSATION: A plan whose terms permit an employee to defer payment of a portion of his salary in return for the employer's promise to pay the salary sometime in the future.

DEPRECIATION: The value that property decreases over time. A tax term covering deductions taken on property.

DIVORCE: A still commonly used term for the termination of a marriage. Now the term used in no-fault to refer to the termination of marriage is *"Dissolution of Marriage."*

DOCUMENT: A legal paper such as an order, will, trust, living will, etc.

DONOR CARD: A written declaration with the intention to allow transplanting of organs upon death.

DOWER: A life estate to which a wife is entitled upon the death of her husband. (See Curtsey)

GLOSSARY

DURABLE POWER OF ATTORNEY: A special grant of authority to act on a person's behalf upon incapacitation of the person.

DURESS: The use of pressure or intimidation by one person against another, causing the other person to do something he would not ordinarily do.

ENFORCEMENT: Legal method of getting one's spouse to pay child support/alimony, or execute any Final Judgment for collection.

EQUITABLE DISTRIBUTION: Distribution of assets in a divorce to the husband and wife according to natural rights and what is a fair share of the marital property, rather than by title.

ESTATE: Everything a person owns or has a financial interest in; the property and possessions of a deceased or bankrupt person.

EXECUTOR: See Personal Representative.

FAIR MARKET VALUE: The price that goods or property will bring with a willing buyer and a willing seller.

FILING: The term used for starting a legal action or for presenting a paper to the court for court recording.

FINAL ARRANGEMENTS: All arrangements made for the disposal and ceremony for a deceased.

FINAL JUDGMENT: The written order of a court on the ultimate issues presented in a case. (Criminal prosecution, dissolution of marriage, law suit)

FINANCIAL AFFIDAVIT: Each party's sworn statement as to his income, expenses, assets, and liabilities.

FRAUD: Intentional deception resulting in injury to another.

GARNISHMENT: Enforcing payment of child support/alimony or a debt judgment by taking of wages, pensions, Social Security, etc.

GRANTOR: A person who gives or transfers property.
GUARDIAN: The person who has the care and management of an estate of an incompetent who cannot act for himself.
HEARING: Any conference held before a judge or hearing officer to decide an issue or motion. **HEIRS:** Persons who inherit by will or if there is no will by statutory law.
HMO: Health maintenance Organization
HOMESTEAD: Any house and surrounding land that is owned and used as a dwelling by the head of a family.
INCAPACITY: A person mentally or otherwise unable to handle his own daily affairs
INHERITANCE: The property that someone receives from a deceased person, either through a will or as stipulated by law.
INSURANCE: A way for a person or a group to protect themselves against a loss that could cause a financial difficulty or disaster.
INTANGIBLE PROPERTY: Property with no physical being except as a writing, such as stocks, bonds, policies, bank books, franchises, goodwill, etc.
INTER VIVOS: A Latin phrase meaning "between living persons." An inter vivos gift, for example, is one that is given while the donor is still alive.
INTESTATE: The condition of having died without a valid will.
IRA: Individual Retirement Account
JOINT TENANCY: A piece of property, real or personal, owned by two or more persons.
JUDGMENT: See Final Judgment.

Glossary

JURISDICTION: The power and authority of a court to hear and rule on a case.

KEOUGH: A plan for the self-employed to save money on a tax-deferred bases for retirement.

LAST WILL AND TESTAMENT: See Will.

LEGAL DOMICILE: The place where an individual has his permanent home or principle establishment.

LETTERS OF ADMINISTRATION: Documents issued by a probate court authorizing the Personal Representative to administer the estate of a person who has died.

LIABILITIES: All the debts that you owe.

LICENSE: The permission granted by a government agency allowing a person or company to engage in an activity that the government wants to regulate.

LIEN: A claim that is placed against property for the purpose of securing a debt owed by the property's owner.

LIFE INSURANCE: A contract under which you pay a sum of money and the insurance company agrees to pay a specific amount of money when you die.

LINEAL DESCENDANT: Refers to descent by a direct line of succession in ancestry.

LIQUID ASSET: Cash or anything else of value that can be easily converted into cash, such as stocks, bonds, or jewelry.

LIQUIDATE: To pay and settle a debt or estate.

LIVING TRUST: A legal document that allows you to transfer title of your property to a trustee, who manages it for you during your lifetime.

LIVING WILL: A written document that informs your family, friends and physicians of your wishes in the event that you are incapacitated by accident or serious illness.

LUMP-SUM: An amount of money or property made payable in one or more payments from a retirement plan or as equitable distribution in a divorce..

MARITAL AGREEMENT: An agreement between the parties as to the distribution of assets, liabilities, and rights of each party.

MARITAL PROPERTY: Any property acquired during the marriage, no matter whose name is on it, and also the increase in value of the separate property.

MARITAL DEDUCTION: An amount allowed for Federal estate and gift tax purposes of certain interests transferred to a spouse.

MEDICARE: Two-part health insurance program administered by the Social Security Administration.

MEDIGAP: Medicare supplement insurance.

MINOR CHILDREN: Children under the age of 18 or dependant children by law.

MISREPRESENTATION: Intent to defraud by implied or express false representation.

MODIFICATION: Any change in the final judgment after it has been entered, such as child support or alimony.

MONEY MARKET ACCOUNT: A type of mutual fund that is invested in highly liquid assets that allows you to write checks.

NET WORTH STATEMENT: A listing of all assets owned minus all the liabilities (Debts) you owe equaling a net-worth.

NET INCOME: The gross income less deductions and exemptions allowed by law.

NO-FAULT: A divorce that is granted without the necessity of finding a spouse guilty of any marital misconduct.

Glossary

NET ESTATE: The portion of an estate subject to Federal and state estate tax.

NOTARY PUBLIC: Someone authorized by state law to administer oaths and attest to the authenticity of a documents and signatures.

OFFER: (FIRM OFFER) A legal term in contracts when someone offers to do or pay something if the other party does something.

ORDER: A written directive stating the decisions of the judge on the issues presented.

PARTIES: A person with a direct interest in the case.

PENSIONS: A program that provides retirement income for a wage owner.

PERSONAL REPRESENTATIVE: A person who manages the affairs of another or an estate.

PERSONAL PROPERTY: All property other than real property.

PETITION FOR DISSOLUTION: A formal application to the court asking that a divorce be granted.

PETITIONER/PLAINTIFF: The party who petitions the court in a law suit.

PLEADING: (Petition) The formal paper setting out the reasons and the relief wanted in a law suit.

POLICY: A contract with an insurance company to compensate you for a specific event such as fire, flood, medical, etc.

POSTNUPTIAL AGREEMENT: An agreement entered into by the parties after marriage.

PRENUPTIAL AGREEMENT: An agreement entered into by the parties before marriage.

PROBATE: The legal process that establishes the validity of a person's *Last Will and Testament* and allows the transfer of assets to the heirs.

PROBATE FEES: The legal fees, Personal Representative's fees and the court costs involved in the probate process.

PROSPECTUS: A statement of the features, history and worth of a security.

PROCESS: (Served) Term used for the formal serving of a court paper, putting a person under the jurisdiction of the court's authority.

REAL PROPERTY: Land including the surface, whatever is attached to the surface, whatever is beneath the surface and the area above the surface.

REDEMPTION: To regain possession by payment of a stipulated price.

RETAINER AGREEMENT: A formal agreement between yourself and your attorney stating costs, legal fees, services, etc.

RESPONDENT/DEFENDANT: The person against whom the action is being taken.

RETIREMENT PLAN: A plan provided by an employer, a self employed person or by an individual deferring taxes and approved by the IRS.

REVOCABLE LIVING TRUST: A trust set up by a grantor that allows him to cancel it at any time.

REVOKE: An affirmative act such as writing "void" across the face of a will or trust.

RULINGS: See Order or Final Judgment.

SECOND-TO-DIE: Usually an insurance or retirement term in use when a plan or policy covers the life of two people and pays an income until the second one dies.

SECURED LOANS: A debt owed to a creditor who holds security that will cover the amount owed.

SELF-PROVING WILL: An affidavit as to the validity of your signature permitting your will to be probated.

GLOSSARY

SEPARATE PROPERTY: Property brought into a marriage, property inherited during the marriage, and property received during the marriage as a gift that you kept in your name and did not commingle.

SETTLEMENT: A resolution of any issue in dispute reduced to writing.

SETTLEMENT AGREEMENT: (Marital Property Agreement) An agreement between the parties as to the distribution of assets, liabilities, and rights of each party.

STAY: The use of a court order to stop a judicial preceding or prevent a judgment from being carried out.

SURVIVOR: A person with an interest in property by reason of his having survived another person who also has an interest in property.

TANGIBLE PROPERTY: Either real or personal property that can be possessed, i.e. home, car, jewelry, etc.

TAX-SHELTERED: A transaction in which a taxpayer reduces his current tax liability by investing in plans that provide deductions from income.

TAXABLE ESTATE: The amount to which the rate of estate tax is applied in order to determine the amount of estate tax payable.

TENANTS-BY-THE-ENTIRETY: The ownership of property, both tangible and intangible, by a husband and wife together.

TITLE: Ownership of property entitling the owner to use, sell, rent, lease, donate or even destroy.

TOTTEN TRUST: A type of bank account in which one person deposits money in his own name, but holds it in trust for another.

TRUSTEE: A person who is authorized by another person to take possession and manage property on behalf of and in the best interest of that party.

TRUSTS: Property, both real and personal, held by one person or entity for the benefit of another.

UMBRELLA POLICY: An extension of insurance which offers protection against almost every possible contingency.

UNIFIED CREDIT: A Federal tax imposed upon the net value of an estate and on gifts over a certain amount.

WAIVER: The voluntary relinquishment of a known legal right or claim.

WILL: A person's declaration of how he desires his property to be disposed of after his death.

INDEX

INDEX

401(k)	21, 84, 107, 155, 183
Financial Statement	35
Loan	107
Records	21
Accidents	8, 32, 65, 183, 289
Automobile	12, 13, 68, 69
Alimony	30, 85, 251, 252, 259, 265, 275, 282
Annuities:	52, 65, 84, 86-88, 283
Benefits	88
Fixed rate	52, 87
Tax-Sheltered(deferred)	52, 85, 86
Variable	52, 85, 87
Assets	59, 63, 69, 151-154, 157-159, 161, 162, 164, 165, 167-169, 183, 188, 189, 192, 240, 251, 256, 258, 261, 270
Financial Statement	35
Marital	201
Net Worth Statement	40
Probate	188, 189, 191
ATM	55, 283
ATM machines	15
Automobile	169, 184, 189, 250, 251
Accident	12, 13, 68, 69
Accounts	183
Financing	106

Index

Insurance 68, 69
Lease 106, 107
Bankruptcy 145, 249-252, 253
   Alimony 251, 252
   Credit 253
   Taxes 247, 251
Banks 118, 120, 197, 198
   Accounts 45, 46, 184, 188, 189, 207, 208, 234
   Certificate of deposit (CD) 21, 46, 184
   Fees 45
   Money Market 46
   Mutual fund 47, 48
   Savings accounts 46
   Scams 223
Burial 90, 151, 178, 179, 182
CDs 21, 46, 55, 87, 184, 284
Children 82, 110, 117, 151, 161, 164-172, 190, 197, 198, 200, 201, 207, 251, 252, 257, 259, 260, 271
   Financial Statement 33
Churning 63, 284
   Long term care 218
COBRA 34
Cohabitation agreements 269-273
   Taxes 270
Con artist 9
Conclusion 277-280
Consumer Information Center 87
Contracts 38, 52, 86, 141-146, 102, 106-108, 137, 219
   Cohabitation agreements 269-276
   Non-contract 146, 156
   Oral 142, 145
   Prenuptial agreements 256, 258, 262, 263
   Requirements 143

Scams 22, 228-230, 235
Written 143-145
Cookie Jar Money 205
Credit Cards and Credit Rating 113-122
Credit 20, 31, 100, 104, 105, 107, 109, 113-122,
149, 197, 207, 250, 251, 285
Credit cards 31, 32, 36, 39, 63, 101, 107, 110, 113-118,
184, 197, 198, 207, 227, 234, 250-252, 285
   Records 20, 21, 24
   Debts 36, 39, 63
Credit rating 101, 106, 107, 116-119, 250, 285
Credit Unions 32, 45, 106, 109, 114, 116, 182
Debts 4, 39, 54, 63, 70, 82, 100, 102, 105, 110,
118, 120, 121, 144, 150, 258-260, 283, 284, 286, 288, 289, 292
   Bankruptcy 251-253, 283
   Credit cards 39, 110
   Cohabitation Agreement 274
   Deceased 174, 183, 188
   Divorce 207
   Financial statements 36, 290
   Prenuptial Agreements 256, 258-260
   Records 21, 24
Deeds 21, 22, 24, 154, 164, 185, 186, 241, 286
   Records 21-24
Divorce 3-5, 119, 148, 161, 170, 195-204, 206, 207,
241, 256-261, 265, 266, 271, 284, 286
   Alimony 259, 265
   Investments 42, 85
   Legal 124, 139, 199, 211, 285
   Probate 189

INDEX

    Records 197, 198, 200
    Social Security 40
    Safety 196, 198
Divorce Financial Specialist 197
Elder law 133
Estate .. 86, 92, 133, 148-162, 165-167, 169, 174, 176, 179,
    183, 185, 188-194, 243, 263, 264, 271, 283, 284, 286-289
    Bankruptcy 247, 251
    Cohabitation Agreement............................... 271, 272
    Legal 124, 131, 179, 291, 294
    Prenuptial Agreement 265
    Records 21-24
    Taxes 64, 70, 84, 151, 166, 167,
        169, 157-162, 192, 243-245, 290, 291, 293
Estate Planning 22, 23, 59, 64. 147-164, 166,
        169, 178, 186, 194, 244, 260, 272
    Insurance 153, 160
    Intestate 151
    Records 149, 151
    Retirement 153
    Taxes 148, 156, 159
    Trusts 149, 151, 156-158, 160-162
    Wills 149-151, 153, 157, 161
Executor (See Personal Representative) ... 63, 167, 168,
        183, 191, 241, 287
Expenses 87, 101, 168, 183, 208, 271, 273
    Financial Statement 38
Federal Government
    EE bonds 52
    Estate Taxes 166, 192, 243, 290, 291, 294
    Gift Tax 192, 243
    Income 21, 30, 31, 37,
        50, 51, 58, 59, 70, 158, 159, 184, 192, 240, 252

Investments 52
Mortgage 102, 105
Social Security .... (see Social Security)
Treasury Bills 53
Treasury bonds 53
Treasury notes 53
Felder, Reoul 259
Final arrangements 177-186
Financial Planner 43
   Agents 44
   Certified Financial Planners (CFP): 44
   Certified Public Accountant (CPA) 44
   Chartered Financial Analyst (CFA) 44
   Chartered Life Underwriter (CLU) 44
Financial Statements 29-40, 42, 82, 154, 184
Forms
   ATTORNEYS 134
   BIOGRAPHICAL INFORMATION 203
   COHABITATION AGREEMENT 274
   COMPARISON CHART 55
   DO YOU NEED LIFE INSURANCE? 70
   ESTATE PLANNING RECORDS 186
   FINANCIAL STATEMENT 37
   FUNERAL AND BURIAL INSTRUCTIONS 185

   FUTURE VALUE MULTIPLIERS 83
   INDIVIDUAL WANTS AND NEEDS 25
   LAST WILL AND TESTAMENT 174
   LETTER CONFIRMING REPRESENTATION...139
   LIVING WILL DECLARATION 176
   MEDICAL INSURANCE
      COMPARISON CHART 220
   MONTHLY EXPENSES 38

INDEX

    NECESSARY RECORDS 24
    NET WORTH STATEMENT 40
    PERSONAL INFORMATION 27
    PRENUPTIAL AGREEMENT 263
    RETAINER AGREEMENT 135
Glossary 281-294
Golodner, Linda F. 225
Home Equity Loan 102, 104, 105, 197
Homeowner's insurance 32, 65-67, 103, 228
Humberto Cruz 120, 121
Illustrations 56, 80, 112, 122, 204, 248, 254, 276
Insurance 3, 45, 57-70, 86, 89, 92, 107, 108, 150, 152, 153, 155, 160, 166, 169, 184, 189, 241, 264, 285, 288, 291
    Accident 12, 13, 32, 65, 183
    Agents 62-64, 216
    Annuity 65, 84, 86-88, 283
    Automobile 20, 33, 34, 39, 68, 69, 110
    Beneficiary 3, 20, 59, 60, 62, 64, 88, 92, 150-153, 160, 166, 181, 183, 189, 260, 271, 283, 284
    Churning 63
    Claim 62, 284
    Credit cards 20, 183
    Deferred 35, 52, 65, 84, 86
    Disability 20, 64, 89
    Financial Statement 32, 35, 36
    Guaranteed replacement 66
    HMO (Home Maintenance Organization)..216, 217
    Homeowner's 20, 32, 38, 65-67, 102
    Life 20, 22, 37, 39, 44, 58-64, 70, 109, 150, 152, 181-183, 186, 189, 243, 260, 271, 284, 289
    Loan 62, 108
    Long term care 213, 218
    Medical 19, 22, 34 37, 38, 210-212, 220, 261, 271

Medigap 212, 213, 290
PPO's (Preferred Provider Plan) 217, 218
Records 19, 22, 24
Renter 38, 67
Second to die 64, 160, 292
Umbrella policy 20, 66, 294
Intestate 151, 168, 189, 288
Investments 2, 21, 24, 34, 35, 41-56, 83, 87, 88, 101,
    154, 167, 168, 170, 188, 211, 240, 242, 259-261, 271
    Tax deferred 33,52,65,82,84
    Government 52, 53
    Insurance 56-61, 64,65
    Mutual funds 44-49, 51
IRA 21, 35, 83, 84, 85, 155, 183, 207, 247, 288
Joint tenancy 151-153, 165,
    166, 171, 183, 189, 197, 270, 271
Landers, Ann 170, 171
Legal 3, 5, 65, 120, 123-140,
    142,143, 146, 148, 149, 153, 155, 162, 165,
    166, 169, 171, 172, 176, 179, 188, 189, 196,
    198, 199, 202, 206, 207, 232, 236, 241, 242,
    250, 266, 272, 282, 285-288, 291,292, 294
    Divorce 5, 124, 139, 199-202
    Elder law 133,173
    Fees 63, 65, 70, 124, 129, 130,
    132, 136, 144, 197, 198, 202, 207, 250, 292
    Prepaid 133
    Procedure 3, 179, 188,
    188, 199, 282, 28-5, 291
    Retainer 127, 129, 132, 135-139, 292
Legal Counsel for the Elderly/AARP 173
Letters of Administration 191, 193, 289
Liabilities 52, 154, 168, 201, 260, 283, 289, 293

INDEX

Financial Statement 30, 36, 40, 287
    Marital 6, 201, 290
    Net Worth Statement 40, 290
Line of credit 104, 105, 197
Living Wills 22, 24, 150,
    151, 164, 166, 172, 185, 286, 289, 290
Loans 36, 37, 39, 47,
    99-112, 114, 116, 119, 120, 251, 252, 286, 292
    Financial Statement 32
    Home 102-105, 156
    Insurance 60, 61, 64, 108, 160, 197
    Lenders 45, 109
    Personal 105-107
McDonald's 13
Medical 25, 70, 100, 104, 110, 156,
    161, 172, 182, 183, 200, 201, 209-220, 271
    Financial statement 32, 38, 39
    Insurance..32, 62, 65, 69, 211, 212, 214, 218, 220, 291
    Long term care 213, 218
    Organ donor card 19
    Records 19, 24
Medicare 186, 212-214, 217, 233, 290
Memories 71-80
Money Market accounts 21, 24, 46, 290
Mortgage 70, 102-105,
    156, 207, 229, 246, 241, 251-253, 264, 273, 283
    Financial Statement 31, 32, 36, 38, 39
    Insurance 58, 63-65
    Records 21, 24
Mutual Fund 44, 45, 47-51, 103, 240, 245, 290
    Fees and costs 48, 49
    Portfolio management 51
    Prospectus 47-51, 53, 292

National Association of Securities Dealers 53
National Association of Securities
    Dealers at 1-800-289-9999 53
National Consumer League's National
    Fraud Information Center 238
National Credit Union Association. 116
National Foundation for Consumer Credit 111
Net Worth 36, 40, 42, 290
Office of Consumer Affair 116
Organ donor card 19, 24, 173
Pension 70, 83, 91,
            144, 155, 182, 183, 186, 241, 288, 291
    Financial Statement 30, 35, 37
    Records 20, 24
Personal Representative .... (see also executor) 151,
        174, 179, 180, 190-193, 243, 264, 287, 288, 291, 292
Portfolio management 51
Power of Attorney 22, 24, 50,
                                                151, 155, 156, 287
Prenuptial Agreement 171, 255-268, 283, 291
Prepaid Legal Services 133
Probate 63, 86, 149, 151-153, 158,
        160, 162, 165, 166, 168, 169, 179, 183, 184, 187-194
Prospectus 47, 51, 53, 292
Records .... (See individual subjects) 2,
        15, 17-28, 35, 62, 73, 90, 117, 119, 132, 164, 181, 183,
                        184, 186, 197, 232, 234, 240, 241
    Public record 149, 150, 162, 188, 190-194
Retirement 35, 42, 52, 81-92, 94, 109, 148, 152, 153,
            155, 164, 183, 189, 212, 241, 247, 261, 291, 292
    401(k) 21, 84, 107, 155,183
    Civil Service 182, 183
    Investments 42, 52, 64, 83, 86-88

Index

IRA 21, 83-85. 155,183
Plans 20, 24, 35, 42, 52, 70, 82-86,
       107, 208, 150, 155, 183, 189, 261, 288-290, 292
    Records 20, 24, 84, 241
    Retirement story 93-98
    SEP 21, 155, 183
Safe deposit box 18, 22, 24, 78, 184, 198
Safety 7-16, 51, 196, 197
    ATM machines 15
    Automobile 10-12
    Home 14, 15
    Personal 8-10, 197
    Restrooms 13
    Scams 9, 16, 229
    Travel 16
Scams 219, 221-233, 235-238
    Auto repair 226, 227
    Charities 232-234
    Credit card 227
    Funeral Plans 236
    Home repair 228-230
    Job offers 235, 236
    Legal services 231, 232
    Packages 237, 238
    Prizes 230, 231
    Sweepstakes 236
    Telephone 222-226, 232. 233
    Travelers 227, 228
    Work at home 234, 235
Security 4, 7-16, 58, 103, 131, 137, 272, 285, 292
    Home 14
    Possessions 13, 14
    Restrooms 13

SEP 21, 155, 183
Shirley Temple 77, 79
Social Security 83, 89-91, 104, 154, 155,
              180, 182, 183, 198, 212, 233, 241, 243, 288
    Divorce 90
    Financial Statement 30, 37
    Medicare 212, 233, 290
    Records 19, 24, 27, 28, 186, 241
Stories
    Saturday Live 75
    When One is Alone 94
Taxes 30, 82, 84, 86, 104, 110, 148, 151, 152, 156-
        162, 166, 184, 188, 192, 193, 234, 239-247, 251, 252
    Bankruptcy 242, 247, 251
    Deferred 49, 50, 52, 61,
              64, 82-87, 91, 104, 107, 289, 292-294
    Capital gains 51
    Estate 132, 133, 148, 151, 152, 154,
              156-162, 167, 169, 192, 243-245, 291, 193, 194
    Gift 192, 214, 243, 245
    Records 20, 21, 24, 35, 90, 184, 241
    Scams 231, 234
    Withholding 30, 31
Travel 9, 13, 16, 20, 94, 101, 115
Trusts 125, 133, 149-154, 156-162,
    165-169, 171, 172, 183, 185, 186, 189, 191, 193, 194, 236,
              241, 243, 245, 258, 260, 283, 286, 289, 292-294
    Financial Statement 35, 37
    Records 20, 22, 24
Unified credit 159, 245, 294
Veteran's Administration 19, 24, 92, 180, 182, 184

INDEX

Wills 2, 22, 24, 42, 124, 125, 133, 139, 149-154, 157, 159-161, 163-176, 180, 181, 185, 186, 188, 189, 191, 193, 194, 241, 258, 260, 264, 265, 272, 260, 273, 282-285, 287-289, 291-294

Workers' Compensation 30

Order Form

- Telephone Orders: call toll-free **800/444-2524**. Have your credit card ready.
- Fax Orders: (941/923-3243) give name, address, telephone number, credit card number and card expiration date.
- Mail Orders: Equity Enterprises, Inc., 5765 Andover Circle, Sarasota, FL 34233

Please send the following books. I understand that I may return any books for a full refund — for any reason, no questions asked. Florida residents, add sales tax.

Suddenly Alone _____ Copies @ $12.95 plus $3.50 shipping and handling.

Divorce: A Practical Guide _____ Copies @ $19.95 plus $3.50 shipping and handling.

Name _____

Address _____

_____

Telephone Number _____

Special autograph instructions _____

_____

Payment: ☐ Check   ☐ Money Order

Call toll free and order now.

Equity Enterprises, Inc.
5765 Andover Circle
Sarasota, FL 34233